ISABELLE GREENE
Shaping Place in the Landscape

Kurt G.F. Helfrich

with contributions by
Isabelle C. Greene
Ines Roberts
Karen Sinsheimer
David C. Streatfield
Hazel White

University Art Museum
University of California
Santa Barbara

LENDERS TO THE EXHIBITION

Dr. John Carleton

Peter Da Ros

Isabelle C. Greene & Associates, Inc.

McDermott-Crockett and Associates Mortuary

Ines Roberts

Pat Scott Masonry

COPYRIGHT © 2005 The Regents
of the University of California
University Art Museum
University of California
Santa Barbara, CA 93106-7130
(805) 893-2951

Published in conjunction with the exhibition, *Isabelle Greene: Shaping Place in the Landscape,* organized by the University Art Museum, University of California, Santa Barbara (March 30 – May 15, 2005).

This project has been made possible through a generous gift from Jon and Lillian Lovelace, as well as support from Bart and Daphne Araujo, Edward B. Cella, Suzanne Duca, Beth Kaplan Karmin, Jack and Sheri Overall, Grace Jones Richardson Trust, Wayne Rosing and Dorothy Largay, and Carol Lapham Valentine. The Museum would also like to extend a special thanks to Pat Scott Masonry and Peter Da Ros for their generosity in helping to create portions of the dry-scape installation within the exhibition.

Catalogue design: Paul Prince, Santa Barbara, CA
Editor: Jane Neidhardt, St. Louis, MO
Printed in an edition of 2000 by Ventura Printing Oxnard, CA

Library of Congress Cataloging-in-Publication Data and Photography Credits can be found on page 94.

Isabelle Greene, Lovelace garden, Santa Barbara

Cover drawing: Isabelle Greene
Mountains, n.d.
© 2005 Isabelle C. Greene
All rights reserved. Used by permission.

Cover photograph: C. Mick Hales
Lovelace garden swimming pool, Santa Barbara
© 2005 C. Mick Hales
All rights reserved. Used by permission.

Title Page photograph: Timothy Hearsum
Isabelle Greene at the Overall garden, Santa Barbara, 2000
© 2005 Timothy Hearsum
All rights reserved. Used by permission.

TABLE OF CONTENTS

DIRECTOR'S FOREWORD

The real voyage of discovery consists not in seeking new landscapes,
but in having new eyes.—Marcel Proust

Last spring I had the pleasure of accompanying Isabelle Greene through one of her favorite gardens. It was a revelation to be able to experience the place through her eyes. Although she knew this garden intimately, when we walked through it together, it seemed as if she was also experiencing it for the first time. What I came to clearly understand was the root of the magic in Isabelle Greene's gardens. It is nothing less than an expression of her continual renewal and re-enchantment with the natural world. Her gardens are, in fact, designed to focus on the nuances of delicate change as well as dramatic transformations, so that they are always, as she states, "about becoming" and not arrival.

The publication of this catalogue marks a major collaborative project between the University Art Museum, University of California, Santa Barbara (UAM) and the Santa Barbara Museum of Art (SBMA), examining the work of innovative landscape architect Isabelle Greene. The Santa Barbara Museum of Art is presenting the illuminated installation *Ines Roberts: Interpretations of Isabelle Greene's Landscapes* (January 29 – May 8, 2005) and the University Art Museum is featuring the exhibition *Isabelle Greene: Shaping Place in the Landscape* (March 30 – May 15, 2005).

This joint venture is the first exploration of Isabelle Greene's approach to landscape design. It has been a pleasure to collaborate with the Santa Barbara Museum of Art in showcasing the talents of this renowned Santa Barbara-based landscape designer, whose groundbreaking work since the mid-1960s has helped to focus attention on environmentally sensitive and sustainable design.

This project presented a great challenge for both our institutions, since there is really no way of replicating the experience of an Isabelle Greene garden in a gallery space. However, we hope to provide viewers with some insight into her creative impulses, working methods, and processes as well as to thoroughly document her considerable achievements. Isabelle Greene's designs have attracted an international following, and we believe that the project, with its multi-dimensional blend of exhibitions, a catalogue, and outreach components will draw a large local, regional, and national audience.

Congratulations to Kurt Helfrich, curator of the Architecture and Design Collection at the UAM, and Karen Sinsheimer, curator of Photography at the SBMA, for their vision and diligence in bringing this project to fruition. We also greatly appreciate the enthusiastic support of Phillip Johnston, director of the SBMA. Finally, we thank Isabelle Greene for her inspired response to the beauty of our natural environment.

We gratefully acknowledge major funding for this project from Jon and Lillian Lovelace. We also appreciate the generous support of Bart and Daphne Araujo, Edward B. Cella, Suzanne Duca, Beth Kaplan Karmin and Ken Karmin, Jack and Sheri Overall, the Grace Jones Richardson Trust, Wayne Rosing and Dorothy Largay, Carol Lapham Valentine, and the Friends of the University Art Museum. The University Art Museum would also like to extend a special thanks to Pat Scott Masonry, Peter Da Ros, San Marcos Growers, Seaside Gardens Nursery, as well as Philip and Carolyn Wyatt, the Sares-Regis Group, and Hollister Center for their generosity in helping to underwrite the costs associated with creating the dry-scape installation within the exhibition.

Bonnie G. Kelm
Director
University Art Museum
University of California, Santa Barbara

Isabelle Greene, Valentine garden, Santa Barbara

INTRODUCTION

The University Art Museum (UAM), University of California, Santa Barbara began exploring the possibility of an exhibition of the work of the landscape designer Isabelle Greene in 2000. Spearheaded by the UAM's former director, Marla Berns, a plan was developed with the Santa Barbara Museum of Art (SBMA) to commission photographs of Greene's best-known gardens in Santa Barbara, to be used to mount concurrent exhibitions at the two institutions: a selection of photographs relating to five of Greene's gardens at the SBMA, and an overview of Greene's career, presented through drawings and photographs relating to ten of her most significant landscapes, at the UAM. Karen Sinsheimer, curator of photography at the SBMA, approached photographer Ines Roberts, who agreed to participate in the project. Berns's subsequent move to the Fowler Museum of Cultural History at the University of California, Los Angeles in 2001 temporarily put the project on hold, but in 2003 Isabelle Greene, Karen Sinsheimer, Ines Roberts, and I resumed those conversations. The result is this catalogue and the two exhibitions, which constitute the first major exploration of Isabelle Greene's work and ideas.

Greene's approach has been to intuit, harness, and enhance the existing natural elements of a particular site to shape a new landscape based on an appreciation of locale. Her self-defined strategy is to use plantings, materials, and designed objects (including walls, gates, and furniture) in tandem with the changing moods of nature—light and shadow, wind, rain, and intense sun—to create a rich interplay of movement. Intimate and personal, Greene's gardens elicit strong emotional responses; she has likened them to memories, strewn within the landscape, left for viewers to decipher. Ines Roberts, with her careful eye, has captured and deciphered many of these "memories" in her beautiful photographs.

Isabelle Greene's career as a designer began in Santa Barbara in the mid-1960s, when ecological concerns began to impact the way landscape architects in the United States shaped their environments. It is no accident that her early interest in environmentally responsive landscape design was connected to Santa Barbara—not only because of her unique knowledge of its rich and varied microclimates, landscapes, and plants, but also because her early work was set against the backdrop of one of the largest manmade disasters to date: the 1969 Union Oil Company platform oil spill in the Santa Barbara channel, which in many ways helped to focus national attention on the need to address environmental issues.

Trained as a botanist and artist, Isabelle Greene brings to her landscape designs—currently numbering over five hundred—a spatial artistry that is difficult to capture through drawings or photographs alone. Conventional models are problematic as well, and it is interesting to note that Greene eschews them except on the most basic level as functional design tools for particular elements. My challenge in curating the UAM exhibition has been to work with Greene to develop strategies that would allow viewers to gain a sense of the elements she uses to shape her landscapes, while at the same time experiencing the richness of these landscapes within a museum setting.

To that end, with the Santa Barbara video production firm Media 27, Inc., we have produced a visual exploration of Greene's most elaborate landscape, the Lovelace garden in Santa Barbara, featuring narration by Greene. In addition, I worked with Greene to create a series of what we have termed dry-scape installations to occur in the Museum's Nachman Courtyard Gallery and Main Gallery. The Nachman Courtyard Gallery installation features specially chosen succulents and stones installed by Greene to give viewers a sense of some of the elements that shape her landscapes. The Main Gallery installation—which, unfortunately, could not be realized beyond initial sketches and model due to fabrication and cost constraints—nonetheless remains, even in proposal form, a powerful statement of the major elements that have shaped Greene's work: the mountains, foothills, and creeks that comprise Santa Barbara's unique watershed system. The installation is further enhanced by materials from Greene's design archives to give viewers a sense of her concerns and interest in sustainable environments. As Greene points out in the interview that appears in this catalogue, such concerns are not new to her work, but are, as they have been all along, intimately connected with her interest the topography, plants, and climate of this place.

It has been my pleasure to work with Karen Sinsheimer and Ines Roberts to showcase Isabelle Greene's creative vision and extend our thinking not only about what a museum is, but also about how to innovatively expand the ways in which we display the work of designers through different media and interpretations. Further, it has been inspiring to work so closely with Isabelle Greene, who is some seventy years young and still growing and developing as a designer.

The catalogue essays by noted University of Washington landscape historian David C. Streatfield and the talented San Francisco-based writer Hazel White, respectively, contextualize Greene's work within Californian landscape design traditions and present a unique exploration of her creative vision and aesthetic through a focus on her Valentine garden. Karen Sinsheimer's essay and Ines Roberts's descriptions and photographs of Greene's gardens present a rich, visual exploration of these magical landscapes. My interview with Isabelle Greene about her proposed dry-scape installation and her thoughts on landscape design, in addition to her artist's statement, provide readers with a personal sense of Isabelle Greene as a multifaceted artist, designer, and individual.

It has been a great pleasure collaborating with all of these individuals. I would like to extend my thanks to each of them, as well as to Todd Anderson, Paulette Bartels, Ralph Clevenger, Lynn Fogel, Rollin Fortier, Mick Hales, Jerry Harpur, Gregory Heisler, Saxon Holt, Bonnie Kelm, Eddie Langhorne, Susan Lucke, Jane Neidhardt, Paul Prince, Chris Scoates, Tim Street-Porter, Victoria Stuber, Mike Verbois, Marie Vierra, and Kathy Williams for helping to make this catalogue and the exhibition possible.

Kurt G.F. Helfrich
Curator, Architecture and Design Collection
University Art Museum
University of California, Santa Barbara

ARTIST'S STATEMENT

Floating above all our preoccupations are the eternal mountains, lofty and majestic—an enormous presence that shapes our lives. They shape our climate, our space, and our watershed too, here at the edge of the continent.

Be aware of those wonderful folds and uplifts, the peaks that snag the mists, those stony bones that stick up through their rugged, green coastal

Isabelle Greene, Pulitzer garden, Santa Barbara

clothing. Be aware also of the voluptuous, sensuous foothills with the arable land fanning out below them. These are our gifts—gifts we notice so little, next to the sea that figures so large in our imagination. And, running down it all, shaping the land as they go, are the many trickles, rivulets, and creeks that pass unnoticed, often throttled underground in pipes, through town, finally to disgorge into the sea.

I love the familiar geography of our western land, so visible, and especially the particulars that shape where I live. I feel so rooted, so intensely belonging on this land. I've tramped it all so thoroughly—examined the vast sweeps and sparkling grains of its deserts, patted its mosses in the mountains, tasted the clear ringing air atop its high peaks, and waded and swum its tarns and rivers. I try to bring my love affair with this land—my sense of attachment to these larger things—into the tiny patches of earth entrusted to my design.

Design—design is all about letting the imagination soar, but keeping a fit to the real picture. It is about holding a window up to the unknown, stepping through it, and firmly grappling with what is found beyond.

Designing a garden—that is all about movement. It is about your movement, passing through it, and enhanced by movement all about:

—flutterings and swayings, given by the movement of zephyrs;

—appearances and disappearances of birds; the scuttling, flying, and crawling of creatures;

—the inexorable and subliminal movement of time—so fundamental to the garden's soul.

Never does a garden arrive—it is forever becoming. Small leaves or unfolding blossoms arrive quickly—you can almost watch. The larger and substantial growth of trees arrives over centuries (by which time other parts of the assemblage have expired). And, throughout, the whole collection moves and changes every season.

All together a garden's movements are more like the movements and passages in a symphony orchestra, except that the whole affair never begins all at once, nor ends at once. Time is the factor which renders to the garden its special character—ethereal, and as endlessly fresh and fragile as spring: you had better be there, or else you might miss it!

Of course there are also weighty elements to garden design: rough, craggy, eternal things like rocks; earthy things, like tractors, men, and camaraderie; imponderable things like "regulatory bodies" and Boards of Directors.

And there are also the thin, gossamer, unpredictable overlays; frost, reflection, shadows, dew. The interplay among these different spectrums provides a garden's intense richness.

To design with all this requires a sense of wholeness—a sense of connections—a serious intent, but with a lively play. The finished product's appearance is only the outcome of the wholeness of the process—the pieces interpreted and stitched together properly. It cannot be programmed; it must be felt, as in a tune.

Final outcomes, then, are a glimpse into meanings far beneath the surface and far beyond our consciousness. They let the visitor in on secrets that are so satisfying, they needn't even be comprehended.

Isabelle C. Greene

Isabelle Greene, Valentine garden, Santa Barbara

Fig. 1 Isabelle Greene, Lovelace garden swimming pool, Santa Barbara

ISABELLE GREENE AND THE CALIFORNIA GARDEN

David C. Streatfield
Professor of Landscape Architecture and Urban Design
University of Washington, Seattle

In 1905 Charles Greene wrote, "There is much being written about gardens and there are those willing to tell me readily enough what to do; but fine gardens are like fine pictures, only it may take longer to paint them with nature's brush." He went on to observe that "California with its climate, so wonderful in possibility, is only beginning to be dreamed of, hardly thought of yet," and to express the hope: "It is not beyond probability that where the sounds of the desert now idly drift and only the call of the coyote breaks the stillness, there may rest a Villa Lante or a Fukagawa garden."[1]

These perceptive comments on the possibilities of creating gardens in California of high artistic quality are revealing, although they give no hint of the short time that would elapse before he and his younger brother would be making their own distinguished contributions to garden design in California. The comments endorse an abstract way of painting with nature's brush that implies endorsement of cultural borrowing, a process garden designers consciously and unconsciously have always used by invoking ideas and forms from other cultures. His celebration of the Villa Lante and Imperial Japanese gardens anticipates the broad range of design references that would come to dominate garden design in the twentieth century, but it does not foresee the value a design approach that celebrates Californian landscapes would come to have. Instead it anticipates the creation of new Edens with unrestrained irrigation and an approach to the outer landscape that, despite the use of local materials, only engages it as a distant prospect to be viewed from the garden.

The history of garden design in California is a classic demonstration of the processes of cultural borrowing. The earliest settlers replicated the designs of the places from which they came. Designers also borrowed widely from other traditions to create imagined paradises that were imposed onto the landscape. Some designers selected other regional cultural traditions to create a sense of regional identity, choosing design modes to match the spectacularly beautiful Californian landscape. This search for a Californian identity continues; it is an evolving rather than a linear process that inevitably reflects changing perceptions and needs.[2]

Until the decline of the modernist tradition in the 1960s, a succession of references occurred to analogous Mediterranean regions, such as Italy, Spain, and North Africa, as well as to England and Japan and to European modernist ideas and forms. The waning of modernism coincided with increasing concerns about environmental issues, particularly the availability of water. Droughts and water rationing reminded Californians of the fact that their state is a dry land. Garden designers were forced to address this issue not as a matter of choice but from necessity.

This is the context of the practice of Isabelle Greene, great-niece of Charles Greene. While her gardens are hard to classify, they are clear demonstrations of regionalist sensibilities of place. The abstract flowing terraces of the Valentine garden (1980-84), planted with interlocking masses of subtly colored plants, was created at a time when water rationing was a serious challenge. It was in fact praised for its creative emphasis on drought tolerance (fig. 2).[3] By contrast, the Lovelace swimming pool (1972-73) is a poetic and apparently naturalistic stream inserted into a gentle woodland setting (fig. 1). The Pulitzer garden (1998-2001) has more obvious cultural origins. Its pure and abstract spaces are like Zen meditations (fig. 3).

Fig. 2 Isabelle Greene, Valentine garden terraces, Santa

The aesthetic range and seemingly effortless inevitability of these gardens assert a strong art of place-making that celebrates the genius loci and, in satisfying programmatic necessities, seeks to foster a new awareness of nature. This essay will place the work of Isabelle Greene in the context of the history of California regionalist gardens by examining her education, her role as an artist designer, and the way that her work intuitively resembles a number of older regional landscape design themes.

EDUCATION

Isabelle Greene's entry into landscape design was largely serendipitous. Born Isabelle McElwain, a grand-daughter of Henry Mather Greene through her mother, she grew up in Pasadena largely unaware of her grandfather's role as a partner in one of the most distinguished architectural firms of the Arts and Crafts period.[4] It is not at all surprising that she knew little about her grandfather's work as an architect and garden designer. In 1922 the office of Greene and Greene was closed and replaced by the firm of Henry M. Greene, which was closed in 1933. The remarkable quality of the oeuvre of these successive firms was neglected by scholars until Jean Murray Bangs interviewed the brothers in the late 1940s.[5] Subsequent scholarship tended to give the younger brother an important but largely technical role as a designer. This interpretation has been reversed in recent scholarship, which

Fig. 3 Isabelle Greene, Pulitzer garden terrace, Santa Barbara

has reclaimed and clarified the significance of Henry Greene's highly refined skills as an architect and landscape designer as being quite distinct from the freer and looser approach of his elder brother.[6]

Isabelle Greene's visits to her grandfather's house created strong impressions of the sensual and elegant rubbed wood detailing in the house. She also remembers being impressed by the rose-embowered trellises in the pergola and on the fences, and by the inevitability of the simple layout of concrete and stone paths beautifully graded to provide comfortable ways of moving through space. This intuitive response to the Greene brothers' strong belief that every part of a garden or house, however small, was a work of art had profound consequences for her work.

Isabelle Greene liked to draw and she remembers how her grandfather gently supported her parents' encouragement of her developing artistic inclinations. She was also fascinated by the natural world, and like many Pasadena residents played in the arroyo experiencing the sounds, smells, and colors of a dry landscape. She maintained a small museum in her family's backyard of mushrooms and bugs kept in formaldehyde. She hiked in the San Gabriel mountains, where she collected shells, stones, birds' eggs, lizards, and wildflowers. These early expeditions initiated a deep understanding and love for this dry landscape.

Greene studied taxonomic botany at the University of California, Los Angeles (UCLA) with the redoubtable Mildred Matthias as one of her teachers. After her marriage, her husband, the botanist J. Robert Haller, harnessed her aesthetic talent for preparing illustrations to his scientific publications. A visit to the Hunt Botanical Library at the Carnegie Institute in Pittsburgh, where two of her drawings were exhibited, impelled her to study art seriously, and she completed coursework for a second degree in studio art.[7] A career as a botanical illustrator seemed inevitable. However, her friend Dr. John Carleton challenged her critical and creative abilities and asked her to design the landscapes for a series of small patios around his psychiatric clinic. Lacking any technical landscape graphic abilities, she labored painfully over the development of alternative designs, but the continual iteration and refinement of a series of overlapping and interlocking planes eventually produced an acceptable design that later received a civic award.

This accidental commission launched her career as a landscape designer. Within a short period she was designing estate gardens in Montecito. Concerned about her lack of technical skills, she enrolled in an evening certificate program in landscape architecture at UCLA. Much of her developing design skills resulted from working closely with and learning from highly skilled landscape contractors. In 1974, to further her professional training, she entered into a partnership with the landscape architect Michael Wheelwright. He reviewed her designs, helped her refine her technical skills, and persuaded her to take the state landscape architecture licensing examination.

It was most fortuitous that her garden design practice began and has continued in Santa Barbara. Santa Barbara County is an ideal place to create gardens, and the region has a distinguished garden tradition that is ecologically and culturally distinct from the rest of coastal California. The equable climate and soils and ideal growing conditions are due to its south-facing location backed by the close presence of the Santa Ynez mountains and the protection of the Channel Islands. By 1893 Baedeker referred to Santa Barbara as the "American Mentone," and it quickly became a place of winter residence, attracting rich, conservative, sophisticated easterners and midwesterners. These cultured individuals commissioned widely admired estate gardens. In 1926, members of the Garden Club of America visited no less than fifty-six gardens in Santa Barbara at its annual meeting in California. In addition, the Santa Barbara community attained an exemplary reputation for planning and design controls intended to protect cultural patrimony and native landscapes.[8]

CREATIVE FREEDOM

Greene's rather casual entry into landscape design is not as unusual as it might appear. It is part of a largely unexamined tradition of California garden designers with unconventional backgrounds and little or no professional training. One group came from the nursery business. The other, to which Greene belongs, includes amateurs such as Francis Townsend Underhill, Lockwood de Forest, and his wife Elizabeth, all of whom practiced as gentlemen/gentlewomen landscape architects, and artists such as Charles Frederick Eaton, Bruce Porter, and most recently Michael de Rose. This group also includes the furniture designer Paul Tuttle, who maintained a very distinguished small practice as an architect and garden designer.[9]

Greene's design practice is similar to this latter group. De Forest and Porter were landscape painters who explored the character and meaning of landscapes by painting regularly. De Forest, like his father, the landscape painter Lockwood de Forest II, who had trained him, painted quick small oil sketches every day until 1925.[10]

This group of designers approached garden design with an artistic freedom unfettered by theoretical conventions or historical design precedents. Greene's artistic freedom was initially reinforced by what she has called a "blissful ignorance" about the history of garden design and the work of other designers. The certificate course in landscape architecture she took did not have a section on landscape history, but her private study of landscape design and artists led to an awareness of the work of landscape architects such as Thomas Church, Roberto Burle Marx, James Rose, and Luis Barragan, and the sculpture of Isamu Noguchi.[11]

REGIONAL GARDEN DESIGN, 1900-1960

In the early twentieth century, Californian designers began to look to the Mediterranean basin to fashion a regional identity. The critic Herbert Croly believed that Italian houses and gardens made more sense in California than anywhere else in America because of the "classic" nature of the landscape.[12] But after 1915 the Spanish Colonial Revival became the dominant architectural mode south of the Tehachapi mountains (the Southland). However, despite the appropriateness of both these design traditions, they were rarely adopted completely. The most successful gardens were relatively small, like the two Andalusian-inspired gardens designed for his own use by George Washington Smith (1918 and 1920). Charles Gibbs Adams' Julian Eltinge garden in Hollywood (1921) combined traditional Hispanic terraced and walled enclosures with native Californian succulents and desert plants.[13]

These designs are in marked contrast to the more common practice of surrounding Italianate and Spanish houses with convincingly detailed paved terraces and pergolas that overlook expansive lawns. The pervasive dominance of the lawn is not surprising, since many Californians were immigrants from regions with green landscapes. They took little trouble to understand or appreciate the arid landscape, except for its climate and beauty. Even Florence Yoch, one of the most sensitive interpreters of Mediterranean design traditions, argued that despite the difficulty of creating and maintaining large lawns, their presence was invaluable.[14] Thus, it was the lawns and their surrounding planting that established the character of garden designs. The typical and expansive practice of planting with a wide range of native, temperate, and subtropical plants spurred Charles Gibbs Adams to caution that "the embarrassment of riches is upon us," adding that "we need to develop restraint and more temperance to resist that danger."[15]

This stylistic pluralism was based on an unquestioned reliance on an unlimited supply of water. It might therefore be expected that the Arts and Crafts movement, with its strong emphasis on regional awareness, would have addressed this issue. But, apart from the consistently dedicated pursuit of drought-tolerant strategies by Kate Sessions in San Diego, the native arid landscape remained a distant although much enjoyed part of the garden prospect. A marriage of vernacular culture and appropriate planting occurred in Sessions's collaboration with Irving Gill on a number of simple courtyard designs abstracted from Spanish Californian precedents. Her small garden designed for Mrs. Robert at Coronado (c. 1916) demonstrated how typical garden spaces could be planted entirely with succulents and cacti to form a delicate tapestry of low, gray, foliage plants with yellow and orange flowers contrasted with the vertical accents of aloes and yuccas.[16] Sessions's progressive contribution and significance is only just beginning to be recognized.

Color was used as an important ordering device by several Arts and Crafts designers, including Bernard Maybeck. Inspired by the colors of the local landscape, Charles Frederick Eaton used picturesque theory to transform his Montecito estate over a period of some twenty years. Seeing the landscape as "golden bronze," he selected a range of plant colors to complement and display this color. Ocean views were broken up so that one never saw too much at once, and the slopes were punctuated by "sky-trees," his term for trees taller than the surrounding tree canopy.[17]

By contrast, Greene and Greene's poetic interpretation of classical Japanese gardens at the Gamble house, Pasadena (1908), combined a restrained color palette with the use of boulders, dragged up from the nearby arroyo, artfully integrated with clinker brick in organic, flowing terrace walls that anchor the house above the subtly undulating grass lawns (fig. 4). The terrace serves as a foreground to the distant mountain views. The symbolic forms of a represented nature were adapted to the needs of leisurely upper-class Americans. Greene and Greene's rural houses and gardens, however, such as the Ladd house, Ojai (1912), establish a much stronger sense of regional identity and are notable for their sensitive siting on rough, boulder-strewn slopes and their lack of lawns (fig. 5).[18]

Fig. 4 Greene & Greene, Gamble house, Pasadena

Fig. 5 Greene & Greene, Ladd house, Ojai

In the 1920s Lockwood de Forest III challenged the conventional use of irrigated lawns by his advocacy of drought-tolerant design. In 1924 he wrote an article for *Garden Magazine* questioning the necessity of lawns. Yet pressure from his clients invariably led to their inclusion in his designs. In articles in the *Santa Barbara Gardener*, he emphasized the selection of drought-tolerant plants and zoning garden spaces by levels of water dependency.[19]

In his own garden in Santa Barbara (1926), he developed a new aesthetic related to the regional landscape. The gardens, flanking the small courtyard house, were filled with rosemary and lavenders, whose subtle gray and blue colors echo the blue haze around the distant mountain tops (fig. 6). The main lawn and the gentle slope above it were organized as the foreground of a vista of the Santa Ynez mountains. It is thus an example of *sharawadgi*, but it differs from most Japanese gardens of this type by appearing to be fully integrated into the regional landscape, completely without spatial boundaries. The colors and textures reinforce a connection to the chaparral-covered mountains. The square lawn, defined by local stone walls, was planted with kikyu grass, which was never irrigated, turning golden brown in the long dry summer. The slope above this was planted with a mixture of low native shrubs and South African bulbs mounded up to cover the garden wall.

Fig. 6 Lockwood de Forest III residence garden, Santa Barbara

The dramatic economic and social changes of the Depression almost inevitably led to the adoption of modernist ideas. After World War II modernism became the dominant design mode in California in both high art and popular gardens. The roles of the garden were redefined. Houses and gardens were functionally and visually united, the garden becoming an outdoor room, often with a swimming pool as a prominent feature. Their abstract character reflected Christopher Tunnard's belief that "the right style for the twentieth century is no style at all."[20]

Fig. 7 Thomas Church, Donnell residence garden swimming pool, Sonoma

Californian modernism embraced a number of different aesthetics involving differing levels of landscape manipulation. Thomas Church employed a fairly limited range of formal devices to fashion a suave minimalism, as in his most famous design, the Donnell garden in Sonoma (1948). The garden sits high in the surrounding ranch land from which it is clearly defined by a curving juniper hedge (fig. 7). Church organized the design as an abstract composition on a single unbroken plane with a lanai, dressing room/guest house, kidney-shaped swimming pool, small panel of grass, angled concrete paving, and redwood decking. The horizontal composition is reminiscent of the overlapping planes of cubist art. The edge of the pool becomes a line in space that simultaneously "implodes" and "explodes," retracing the forms of the abstract sculpture by Adeline Kent at the center of the pool, and the broad, sweeping, oxbow bends of the river in the valley below.[21] The superlative control of these elements creates a "visual endlessness" of multiple viewpoints as one moves through the space. Church insisted on controlling visual complexity: "All is calculated to give complete restfulness to the eye. If the eye sees too many things it is confused and the sense of ease is obliterated."[22] The carefully pruned sculptural oak trees and the small panels of grass and zoysia grass provide a counterpoint to the unbroken ground plane. Church's greatly simplified plant palette decisively rejected the refined planting characteristic of the 1920s, and was intended to be easily maintained.

Less conservative clients commissioned more overtly experimental designs that employed an unrestrained use of new materials and elaborate, interlocking, abstract patterns on the ground and in vertical elements such as screens.[23] New materials such as asbestos-cement, plastic, and aluminum in panels and poured concrete paving were used to express modernity, and art was frequently boldly incorporated onto structural features.

Richard Neutra's Warren Tremaine garden, Montecito (1947-1948), represents a softer modernism. His theory of bio-realism is based on the animistic ideal of oneness with the natural world. "An ensemble of plants that can keep natural company" was selected to carpet the ground plane as a setting for his abstract architecture.[24] The house, grounded in nature, appears to float above a carpet of massed succulents, hillocks of zoysia grass, and aloes, with yuccas and cacti providing a vertical counterpoint. Nevertheless, this oasis of drought-tolerant planting was surrounded by a pastoral setting of expansive lawns no different from his earlier designs.

REGIONAL GARDEN DESIGN, 1960-PRESENT

In the 1960s California began to play a leading national role in addressing a range of environmental issues. This coincided with the waning popularity of the modernist garden tradition. Leading modernist designers such as Garrett Eckbo, Robert Royston, and Lawrence Halprin turned away from garden design to take on the design and planning of large urban, commercial, and institutional commissions. By the time Isabelle Greene initiated her design practice, the garden was no longer the place of potent design experimentation that it had enjoyed since the late 1930s.

Garden design shifted in different directions. Historicist themes were taken up by some designers, while others adapted modernist forms to new ends. Modernist ideas about function remained unquestioned, but minimalist, abstract forms were softened through the use of a wider plant palette. The less adventurous garden designs of Owen Peters and Courtland Paul used tile, brick, and grass, rather than concrete. Plywood, aluminum, plastics, and other industrial materials were supplanted by more earth-toned materials. Swimming pools and spas were frequently designed without diving boards and grab bars, being conceived also as reflection pools. Planting became much softer. Trees were no longer treated as isolated living sculptures, carefully positioned against brightly colored fences. Instead, shrubs and trees were used as space-defining elements.[25]

In the 1970s and 1980s a younger group of designers with diverse backgrounds, including Isabelle Greene, initiated garden design practices that explored a more consistently regional approach. Designs by the late Robert Fletcher, Nancy Goslee Power, and Chris Rosmini can be found in the Southland; Ron Lutsko's designs can be found in the San Francisco Bay area. Rosmini, who began her practice at the same time as Greene, has a background in classics, and her work reveals an equally formidable plantsmanship. The other designers opened their offices in the early 1980s. Fletcher and Lutsko were trained as landscape architects, and Power was trained as an interior designer.[26]

In very different ways each designer's work creatively acknowledges the dry nature of the landscape. Each uses lavish planting, not seen since the 1920s, to create rich and subtle effects. Fletcher and Rosmini create dazzling effects without resorting to much formal structure. They use drought-tolerant plants and low shrubs as an alternative to grass lawns. Power, who lived in Italy for several years, frequently makes overt references to Italian garden traditions by using simple formal parterres, paved areas, and terraces. Lutsko approaches garden design with a deep understanding of local plant communities, which he combines with a simple, modernist handling of space, inspired by the work of Dan Kiley.[27]

A severe drought in the 1970s forced designers to address the necessity of using drought-tolerant plants. Conferences were held on xeric landscaping and a number of books appeared that focused on dry landscapes. Owing to its unwillingness to participate in the state water plan, Santa Barbara County enforced water rationing in the early 1980s. Greene's early garden designs already recognized and celebrated the colors and character of the semi-arid landscape, so that by the early 1980s her work was hailed as prophetic, despite her insistence that drought tolerance has never been a driving factor in her approach to design.[28]

Today, dry gardening and issues of sustainability have come to dominate thinking about gardens. In 1986 Bob Perry redesigned the grounds of Charles Fletcher Lummis's house, "El Alisal," in Highland Park as a public demonstration of dry gardening practices.[29] This emphasis on ecological concerns, especially water conservation, has led to the garden re-emerging as a place of design experimentation, with the particular challenge of addressing environmental issues in creative and artful ways. It is in this area that Isabelle Greene has made important contributions.

ISABELLE GREENE'S IDEAS AND DESIGN APPROACH

Greene's early work was an artistic exploration free of the influence of other designers. After her certificate course she became interested in the work of a number of designers. James Rose fascinated her with his innovative ways of creating transparency, and the way in which he used angled railroad-tie stairs to emphasize the underlying forms of the topography. Roberto Burle Marx's bold and painterly use of broad, interlocking masses of color inspired her to abstract the forms of topography and plant communities. Isamu Noguchi's sculpture revealed the potential of this art form as a source of inspiration for garden design.[30]

Fig. 8 Isabelle Greene with Andy Neumann, Architect, Overall garden, Santa Barbara

Greene's ideas about design derive from her training as an artist. She believes strongly in exploration and intuition as a way to give primacy to one's feelings and open up new perceptual possibilities. Her exploratory designs are based on an appreciation of landscape color derived from her lifelong interest in hiking and close study of the rhythms of dry landscapes (fig. 8). Her plant palette includes lavender, gray, sage, and light green. Her preference for blue-gray and khaki is often offset by silver highlights. Carefully graded sequences of gray are used to heighten a sense of distance. She has strongly criticized unappreciative reactions to dry landscapes, but she has been willing to address clients' preferences for lushness by using rich colors to substitute for grass and including lawns where she feels that they are appropriate.

Formulated in 1987, her design philosophy of "earthenscape," a term she devised to describe unplanted space or to signify non-living materials, emphasizes elements that visually complement the adjacent plants and have rich color. "The concept for a garden coming into being can happen almost instantaneously, but the realization of that concept is a continuous *growing* into *being,* a process that never stops." A garden is a form of living sculpture with fixed and changing parts. This forces the designer to approach design with a willingness to allow inevitable changes to occur. "I brush garden canvases with a play of light, the sharp greens of foliage, and the soft colors of blossom, sheets of rock, or water or tinted concrete. I push shelves of slanted Salal foliage against the vertical lines of delphiniums and hope the gardener can maintain it over time; for six months or two years or much more, I keep the requirements firmly in mind and coach the owners and gardeners until all is working." Random processes cause her to marvel at the conjunctions of planned and unplanned events, and she celebrates the role of the owners in finishing the garden as art.[31]

Greene is strongly attracted to Oriental gardens, which she admires for their simplicity and restraint. The Pulitzer garden presented the challenge of reworking and unifying the areas surrounding a house designed in the 1960s. The client had significant allergy problems, which was a driving factor for the design. Greene's design comprises a tightly organized series of spaces planted with non-pollen bearing plants, such as cacti, aloes, and bamboo. She reduced the size of the motor court and converted the large porte-cochere into a lanai. The most remarkable aspect of the Pulitzer garden is her conversion of a rectangular panel of grass into an abstract composition of gravel and standing stones that is like a Zen meditation, its sculptural nature inviting comparison with Noguchi's work (fig. 3). Her poetic reference to Zen gardens contrasts with the ways in which Topher Delaney, a San Francisco Bay area designer who employs abstract forms and strong colors, and Nancy Goslee Power draw from cultural traditions. Power, who lived in Italy, frequently makes explicit references to some of its design traditions. Delaney develops her garden narratives by selecting from cultures that intrigue her and her clients.[32] While the Pulitzer garden achieves the meditative effect of a Zen garden with some similar uses of materials, Greene's overall design responds primarily to the architecture of the house rather than to another cultural tradition.

Like many of her peers, Greene has re-examined the modernist convention of an unbroken ground plane, which is often ecologically inappropriate. Many of her gardens are situated at the base of the Santa Ynez mountains, where the steep topography impels different solutions. The principal part of the Valentine garden lays one story below the house. The abstract patterns of its terraces, inspired by Indonesian rice paddies, were intended to prevent a feeling of tipping downward. When viewed from below, the battered and tinted concrete walls, formed by rough cedar shake formwork, provide a strong visual base for the house.

Flowing water is the organizing theme of the Valentine garden. Water originates in a small Zen garden, proposed by the client, by the front door. From there it flows into a recirculating pool defined by irregular Yosemite black slate stones. This miniaturized lushness changes into the suggestion of a band of water gently flowing around the house through a symbolic use of irregular slate panels; it continues through buff-colored gravel at the side of the house, and then winds across the lower terraces. The planting on

Fig. 9 Isabelle Greene with Andy Neumann, Architect,
Overall garden swimming pool, Santa Barbara

the terraces of gray and blue-gray ground covers and grasses suggests water meandering slowly and spilling over into the symbolic stream. Upright aloes and yuccas provide bold, formal contrast (fig. 2).

The Overall garden (1998-2001) is set on an extremely dramatic site against a mountain wall, commanding sweeping panoramic views out over the ocean. Greene's design marries the house to the site by establishing an effortless descent from the house through a series of angled stairs winding down among boulders to a broad, level platform that forms a bold gesture in the seemingly undisturbed natural setting of oak trees with large sweeps of ceanothus. This design invites comparison with Thomas Church's Donnell garden for the similar way in which the pool acts as a visual focus, simultaneously bringing the eye back into the site and directing it outward to the broad panorama of the ocean. The gentle fall of the water over the outer edge of the pool furthers the effect of water suspended in space, a favorite device of James Rose, and directs the eye outward. The suspended sheet of water is complemented by the silhouette of a graceful eucalyptus tree that is just over the property line, but which appears to be a calculated element of the visually dramatic ensemble (fig. 9). With this powerful design, Greene effectively demonstrates an alternative to the modernist preference for a single, uninterrupted plane.

PROFESSIONAL PRACTICES

Greene's work bears similarities to a number of common practices from the 1920s. Designers such as Lockwood de Forest, Edward Huntsman-Trout, Thomas Church, and Ruth Shellhorn paid considerable attention to their clients, finding inspiration in satisfying their various functional and spiritual needs. The importance of this approach is summed up in the title of Church's book, *Gardens Are for People*.[33] While this was an important element of the modernist emphasis on function, in practice it was frequently overridden by aesthetic considerations. With remarkable candor Garrett Eckbo, for example, told the author in retrospect that he had explored design themes that were of little or no interest to his clients.[34] By contrast, Greene, like many older designers, maintains close relations with her clients, often remaining friends with them for decades.

The Lovelace garden is Greene's longest association and has extended over thirty years. This rivals similarly long associations, such as that of Lockwood de Forest and Wright Ludington at "Val Verde," which extended from 1926-1948.[35] One of the greatest values of such long associations is the ability to evaluate the success of the design, and edit or make appropriate adjustments. The swimming pool was the first of Greene's Lovelace designs, which began in 1972 (fig. 1). This scheme for a natural pool in the woodland to the side of the house was unusual in its placement away from the lawn and the terraces

Fig. 10 Isabelle Greene, Lovelace garden gate, Santa Barbara

Fig. 11 Isabelle Greene with Andy Neumann, Architect,
Lovelace garden poolhouse bench, Santa Barbara

around the house. Its fluid and natural character was devised by plotting the intersecting canopies of the surrounding group of live oaks. Its space is defined by a series of large boulders moved from elsewhere on the site to foster the illusion of a natural body of water in the woods. The legally mandated protection around the pool area was effected by inserting a wittily designed pair of wrought iron gates between two large boulders, incorporating the butterfly designs that appear on each house shutter (fig. 10). Greene later collaborated with the architect Andy Neumann to design and site a small Japanese-inspired bathhouse and sauna overlooking the pool. The design of the surrounding deck reveals Greene's effortless ability to fashion abstract and exquisitely crafted details. This small feature recalls the craftsmanship of her grandfather's era (fig. 11).

Equally important to earlier designers was the continuing involvement with garden maintenance. In the 1920s landscape architects typically advised on the hiring of gardening staff and often provided instruction manuals that detailed design intentions, pruning (which was regarded as an art by most designers), and other maintenance practices such as horticultural requirements. Greene also honors this practice.

Greene signs a small number of her commissions with her initials in stone, like a petroglyph. She does not hide necessary horticultural accouterments such as hoses and hose bibs, but treats them as critical design features. She has developed a range of designs, including different bird designs to adorn hose faucets, and scooped shallow depressions from boulders to create a place for coiled hoses (fig. 12). These elegant solutions are unusual in current designs, but are similar to those used by older designers, such as Florence Yoch.

Fig. 12 Isabelle Greene, Petersen garden, Santa Barbara

CONCLUSION

Isabelle Greene's contributions to regionalist Californian gardens are considerable. She has fashioned a regionally specific art of place that is derived from the landscape and the particularities of clients' needs. Unlike the modernist garden in which "art" was placed in "nature," her art is completely embedded in nature.

Her unusual background in botany and art enabled her to carry forward the traditions of a small group of lesser-known, but historically significant, artist and landscape architects who challenged conventional norms and created innovative gardens. Her gardens recall older themes of regional garden design, such as acknowledging and celebrating the ecologies of dry landscapes, respecting the client, and paying meticulous attention to the smallest details (fig. 13), ensuring that each element is a work of art.

The Lovelace garden (fig. 1), Valentine garden (fig. 2), Pulitzer garden (fig. 3), and Overall garden (fig. 9) are unquestionably among the finest examples of western garden art of the late twentieth century. They stand apart from the work of her peers in their subtle and understated reference to other cultural design traditions, and in the way that critical environmental issues such as drought tolerance and sustainability are addressed by literally "painting with nature's brush."

Fig. 13 Isabelle Greene, Valentine garden terrace steps, Santa Barbara

NOTES

[1] Charles Sumner Greene, "California Home Making," Tournament of Roses Edition, *Pasadena Daily News* (January 1905): 27.

[2] See Marc Treib, "Aspects of Regionality and the Modern(ist) Garden in California," in Therese O'Malley and Marc Treib, eds., *Regional Garden Design in the United States* (Washington D.C.: Dumbarton Oaks Research Library and Collections, 1995), 5-42.

[3] See Russell A. Beatty, "Greening of the Brownsward," *Pacific Horticulture* 49 (Winter 1989): 30-40

[4] See Randell L. Makinson, *Greene and Greene: Architecture as a Fine Art* (Salt Lake City: Gibbs M. Smith, 1998) and Edward R. Bosley, *Greene and Greene* (London: Phaidon, 2000).

[5] Jean Murray Bangs, "Greene and Greene: The American House Owes Simplicity to Two Almost-Forgotten Brothers Who Showed Us How to Build with Wood," *Architectural Forum* 89 (October 1948): 80-89.

[6] See Bosley, *Greene and Greene,* 176-189.

[7] *Catalogue of an Exhibition of Contemporary Botanical Art and Illustration, 6 April to 1 September, 1964* (Pittsburgh: Hunt Botanical Library, Carnegie Institute of Technology, 1964), 31.

[8] See Mac Griswold and Eleanor Weller, *The Golden Age of American Gardens: Proud Owners, Private Estates, 1890-1940* (New York: Harry N. Abrams. 1991), 324, 311.

[9] Garden designers from the nursery trade include A.E. Hanson, Raymond Page, Paul Howard, Paul Theine, and Benjamin Morton Purdy. For more on Francis Underhill, see David Gebhard, "Francis T. Underhill," in Robert Winter, ed., *Toward a Simpler Way of Life: The Arts and Crafts Architects of California* (Berkeley: University of California Press, 1997), 103-110. For more on Bruce Porter, see David C. Streatfield, *California Gardens: Creating a New Eden* (New York: Abbeville Press, 1994), 88, 91-93, 96-100, 262. For more on Lockwood de Forest, see William F. Peters, *Lockwood de Forest,*

Landscape Architect, Santa Barbara, California, 1896-1949 (unpublished Master's thesis, University of California, Berkeley, 1971). For more on Michael de Rose, see Kathryn Masson, *Napa Valley Style* (New York: Rizzoli, 2003), 164-175. For more on Paul Tuttle, see Kurt Helfrich, "The Architectural Projects of Paul Tuttle," in *Paul Tuttle Designs* (Santa Barbara: University Art Museum, University of California, 2003), 158-183.

[10] Lockwood de Forest used the title Lockwood de Forest Jr., although he was Lockwood de Forest III. See Peters, *Lockwood de Forest, Landscape Architect, Santa Barbara, California, 1896-1949.* For his father's plein-air sketches, see Joseph R. Goldyne, *Lockwood de Forest: Plein-Air Oil Sketches, May 17 to July 27, 2001* (New York: Richard York Gallery, 2001).

[11] Streatfield--Greene interview, Santa Barbara, California, March 19, 2004 (unpublished).

[12] Herbert Croly, "The Country House in California," *Architectural Record* 34 (December 1913): 483-519.

[13] For more on George Washington Smith's garden of 1916, see *Architect and Engineer* 71 (December 1922): 49-68, 75-78. For more on his garden of 1920, see *House Beautiful* 51 (January 1922): 28-29. For more on Charles Gibbs Adams' garden for Eltinge, see Elmer Grey, "The residence of Julian Eltinge, Esq, Los Angeles, Cal., Pierpont and Walter S. David, architects," *Architectural Record* 49 (February 1921): 98-113.

[14] Florence Yoch, unpublished notes for a book on garden design, collection of Mrs. Robert Ward, Portola Valley, California.

[15] Charles Gibbs Adams, "Our Architectural Tragedy," *California Southland* 10 (July 1928): 28-29.

[16] See Mrs. Francis King, *Pages from a Garden Note-Book* (New York: Scribner's Sons, 1915), 196-203.

[17] For Bernard Maybeck's use of color, see Dianne Harris, "Making Gardens in the Athens of the West: Bernard Maybeck and the San Francisco Bay Region Tradition in Landscape and Garden Design," in O'Malley and Treib, *Regional Garden Design in the United States,*

43-68. Charles Frederick Eaton's terms are quoted in Gustav Stickley, "Nature and Art in California," *The Craftsman* 6 (July 1904): 370-390.

[18] See Bosley, *Greene and Greene*, 115-127, 165-166.

[19] Lockwood de Forest, "Do Lawns Belong," *Garden Magazine* (May 1924): 232. Lockwood and Elizabeth de Forest edited the *Santa Barbara Gardener* from 1925-1942. See especially "Down with the Water Bill," *Santa Barbara Gardener* 1 (August 1926): 1.

[20] Christopher Tunnard, "Modern Gardens for Modern Houses," *Landscape Architecture* 39 (January 1942): 57-64.

[21] Marc Treib offers a different interpretation of the forms of the swimming pool. He suggests that Jean Arp's and Joan Miro's paintings were the inspiration. See Treib, "Aspects of Regionality and the Modern(ist) Garden in California," 39-41.

[22] Thomas D. Church, "Peace and Ease," *House Beautiful* 94 (October 1952): 209.

[23] See Garrett Eckbo, *Landscape for Living* (New York: Architectural Record with Duell, Sloan, and Pearce, 1950).

[24] Richard Neutra, *Mystery and Realities of the Site* (Scarsdale: Morgan and Morgan, 1951), 10-12.

[25] This is a largely unexamined period of garden design in California. For the best discussion, see Jere Stuart French, *The California Garden and the Landscape Architects Who Shaped It* (Washington, D.C.: Landscape Architecture Foundation, 1993), 196-211.

[26] See Patricia Thorpe, "Digging for a California Style: Climate, Terrain and History Shape the Regional Approach of Three Garden Designers," *House and Garden* 164 (November 1992): 189-204. See also Page Dickey, "Ron Lutsko," in her *Breaking Ground: Portraits of Ten Garden Designers* (New York: Artisan, 1997), 120-137.

[27] See Dickey, *Breaking Ground*, 126-133. Ron Lutsko Jr., "Designing a Garden of Native Plants," *Pacific Horticulture* 49 (Summer 1988): 40-46, Lutsko, "Designing the Dry Garden: Perennials for the Sun," *Pacific Horticulture* 50 (Summer 1989): 30-38, and Dan Kiley and Jane Amidon, *Dan Kiley: The Complete Works of America's Master Landscape Architect* (Boston: Little, Brown and Company, 1999).

[28] See Bob Perry, *Trees and Shrubs for Dry California Landscapes: Plants for Water Conservation* (San Dimas, CA: Land Design Publishing, 1981), and Beatty, "Greening of the Brownsward," 36-37.

[29] See Streatfield, *California Gardens,* 246-239.

[30] Streatfield--Greene interview, Santa Barbara, March 20, 2004. See also James C. Rose, *Creative Gardens* (New York: Reinhold Publishing Corporation, 1958), and P.M. Bardi, *The Tropical Gardens of Burle Marx* (New York: Reinhold, 1964).

[31] Isabelle Greene, "A New Division. The Spatial Arts," *Santa Barbara Arts* (June/July 1987): 5-8.

[32] See Thorpe, "Digging for a California Style." For more on Topher Delaney, see Marcia Tanner, "Topher Delaney's Faith in the Future," *Garden Design* 10 (May-June 1991): 71-78.

[33] Thomas Dolliver Church, *Gardens Are for People: How to Plan for Outdoor Living* (New York: Reinhold Publishing Corporation, 1955).

[34] Streatfield--Eckbo interview, Berkeley, California, March 1974 (unpublished).

[35] See Peters, *Lockwood de Forest*, 46-60.

Isabelle Greene, Valentine garden, view of entrance to house from Zen garden, Santa Barbara

LINES TO PARADISE

Hazel White

> *What really thrills me are things in the landscape that run through my body, that put me in a position of physical alertness, almost as if danger were present, like the light before a storm. The mind comes alive and the body, too. Is that "paradise," to be so stirred? Yes, that's it—"to be so stirred."—Isabelle Greene*

When I arrived, I felt immediately alert, in a way I could not understand.

The small road from Santa Barbara to Montecito curves along the hillside toward the Valentine residence through the shadows of coast live oaks. The blue-yellow air, a mix of ocean fog and mountain heat, is scented with bay leaves. At a bend in the road, honey-colored boulders form humps on the dusty land; farther on, a creekbed carries a river of sun-baked boulders and dead leaves. This land between the Santa Ynez mountains and the Pacific Ocean was home to the padres who founded the Santa Barbara Mission in 1786. In caves in these mountains, the Chumash Indians elaborately painted images of their world as it connected to the universe. This land is also the home of landscape architect Isabelle Greene. She grew up about ninety miles south, in Pasadena, close to a landscape much like this; she has lived in Santa Barbara, hiking and working on the slopes of these mountains, for forty-eight years.

Isabelle Greene, *Foothills*, charcoal on paper, n.d.

The car pulls out of the shade, crosses a gully on a white-walled bridge, and slips into a graveled entrance court filled with light. Around the court rise tall, white retaining walls and the sides of a modernist white-box house with louvered shutters and a log pergola porch. Across the space, light rolls uninterrupted, glancing off the walls, cartwheeling over the gravel. Arriving is thus a deliverance of sorts. It is a joy, physically felt, to leave behind the tangle of woodland shadows and crossing tree trunks and let your eyes slide over architectural planes. A clean separation like this between nature and modern architecture inspires some landscape architects—those who work with the garden as a logical extension of the house, playing with its crisp lines, inventing spaces that speak to the indoors. One of the possibilities of landscape architecture, writes Elizabeth B. Kassler, is that it "can offer an experience of architecture."[1] But Greene's inspiration comes mainly from the

California mountains and valleys. She finds geometric lines dull; you will see very few of them in her work. Instead, her work offers us landscape architecture's other possibility, "an experience of universal nature." Greene returns us to a primordial place, where we meet nature kinesthetically, as pure sensation—a place, she says, that we barely remember "deep in the recesses of our minds."[2]

Here at the entrance, Greene sweetens the architectural geometry with organic lines that torque toward the sun. Near the house entrance, two white-trunked eucalyptus trees—*Eucalyptus citriodora*, a favorite tree of Greene's—rise as thin verticals into blue sky beside the white walls, softening them. A flame vine, pruned to a series of lines, loops along a wall top. The car tires crunch to a halt at a peeled log wheel-stop lying in the gravel.

There is warmth and light all around, white walls and soft leaf colors, a restrained elegance without pretension. But, more than that, there is the beginning of a sense that something is at stake. I cannot find the source of it, though I note the absence of standard landscape architecture tricks—no tension or grand spectacle, the qualities most often used to create excitement. When Greene started this garden in 1980, sixteen years into her career, she was not a licensed landscape architect (nor was she ever much influenced by her later study of landscape architecture). She had learned construction as a teenager, helping her family build from scratch a concrete-block ranch house in the Granada Hills, designed by her architect grandfather, Henry Mather Greene. When she designed the Valentine garden, still her most famous garden to date, Greene's formal training was in botany and studio arts.

Isabelle McElwain (Greene) at Granada Hills house construction site, 1952

In subsequent visits to the Valentine garden, and to many other of Isabelle Greene's gardens, I have studied how she shapes the land and noted her sensitivity to the natural world, as well as the signature health of the plants in her gardens and the botanical perfection of their placement. I have come to recognize how she choreographs grays and greens and arranges rocks to evoke the native southern California landscape. Yet of most interest to me is what Greene's work summons in the imagination and the capability of her residential gardens not only to stir the senses but to stir our connection to the land outside the garden, to connect us to nature.

TOPOGRAPHICAL PLAY

The topography of the Valentine garden—the configuration of its land surface, the conjuring by line and volume of a sense of place—is a created one that comes alive in the viewer's mind. Plans show that the entrance court and the house sit on two shelves cut out of the hillside, and the main garden flows down the slope behind the house. A side garden (actually a roof garden) takes you from the house entrance around to a spacious patio, which serves as the grand access to the garden from indoors. From the patio, stairs descend to the main garden. All this is so, and yet it seems false to describe it this way. The experience of the garden denies the facts of it.

The geometry of the place angered Greene when she first saw it. She thought the compound of sleek architecture—white house surrounded by white garden walls—separated Mrs. Valentine from nature:

> Mrs. Valentine seemed such a genuine person who loved her site and her oaks that the thought of her being cut off from what was around her by all these geometric walls was pretty hard on me.

In this garden, more than in any garden before or since, Greene had to struggle mightily to reconnect the garden to the natural world beyond it. She succeeded in diminishing the solidity of the garden walls and conjuring an experience of what twenty years later she would call "paradise." The Valentine garden remains the purest expression of her creative will.

From the entrance court, I pass through a gate, and then proceed on a straight concrete path to the front door across a dry stream. The path, set by the architect Paul Gray, has been transformed by Greene into a bridge across a tiny piece of natural landscape. The stream swirls into being in raked circles in the gray gravel beneath a similarly swirling mayten tree and seems to go under the path to emerge again in a plain of tan gravel, over which it flows to the shore of a pond, which reads like a lake, in the side garden.

Isabelle Greene, Valentine garden, Zen garden pond, Santa Barbara

Blue-gray slate stepping stones flow from the bridge into the garden, which is reminiscent of a Zen garden. I take two giant steps forward. The manipulated scale—strips of gray gravel as stream, pond as lake, lichen-covered rocks as mountains—skews my sense of time as well as space. It is as if I am released from the familiar world and its gradations of measurement and lofted into a private, weightless, transcendent way of seeing. "Once we attend to the miniature world, the outside world stops and is lost to us," writes Susan Stewart.[3] Time seems "arrested;" we lose ourselves in the presentness of the details, which increase in significance, she says, the more they are reduced in scale.

Ahead, a beach of glinting slate shards borders the lake. There is a buzz rising off the beach—like a hint of rhythm ricocheting in the air. Light is revving up the atmosphere: it is projecting the blue summer afternoon sky onto the water, refracting off the slate stones onto the papyrus stems, drifting among the papyrus tops. In my mind, I am dissolved into the air, lifting and falling with the leaves. The garden walls, reflected hazily in the pond, seem irrelevant.

Isabelle Greene, Valentine garden, Zen garden pond, Santa Barbara

Greene's small pond has become the most photographed garden water feature in the past two decades. Images of it have appeared in international design books and the London *Sunday Telegraph Magazine*. The heart of the scene lies across the water, under the papyrus. A spring bubbles there beneath the flame vine, and sunlight pours across the plain and lake, making the moving water glitter. Even looking at a secondhand image, a photograph in a magazine, what takes form is the archetypal garden: "the protected and enchanted miniature of the beloved earth that supplies all our needs."[4]

Isabelle Greene, Valentine garden, Zen garden stone stream, Santa Barbara

Once the path leaves the pond and winds into the presence of an old oak growing beyond the garden wall on the hillside, it becomes processional. The garden is darkest here beneath the oak branches. Light pricks green onto the tops of the boulder-mountains; ferns grow in the crevices like forests of fir. A dwarf purple maple, supremely healthy, waves its thin leaves on the breeze. The oak leaves flutter in a conjoining, rocking rhythm. The silence between the movements seems taut with reverence.

At the house corner, under the oak, the stepping stones and stream turn along the side of the house and head toward the patio at the back. The stream laps at the stepping stones, slips like an oxbow lake against the roots of a pomegranate tree, and then rides through a gorge between slabs of stone under your feet. Greene lays down gravel and stone to conjure mountain crevices, dry washes, and alluvial plains. She knows the textures, shapes, and colors of the land in this part of California as a botanist and as an artist, and she can mold a natural topography with great ease. As a child, she spent warm afternoons like this one watching lines of water advance through arroyos and collect in rock pools. Her paternal grandmother, Clara McElwain, encouraged outdoor play; Greene built miniature landscapes in the mud.

> *I'm in my sunsuit, out in the sunshine, squatting, holding the hose, filling up the little mud dam I just made and watching the water trickle on down. I had created a village or something—I remember the slab of mud that created the wall of the dam. It was quite evenly shaped, a mathematical curve with a nice smooth inside and an absolutely flat top. That's glued in my memory, standing there with my feet in the mud and patting those shapes.*

In the late 1960s, a few years after starting landscape work to earn her living, Greene was creating ceramics in the studio arts program at the University of California, Santa Barbara (UCSB) with uncannily beautiful, deeply perceived organic lines. Still she loves mud and molding. Her favorite moment in landscape-making is not when the garden has been planted—although she is likely to weep with joy when she sees the first birds land on the new plants—but when the land is sculpted:

> *When it is clean and freshly finished, and it conforms, it shows the vision, only in tones of brown, nothing else and nothing upon it. That's the glory moment, right there.*

One day she was standing in a dry creekbed feeling enlivened by the shapes of a newly raked landscape she had made when she saw a shiny line of water slipping through the stones. "I wondered, did I do all of this work for this, to be here as I was as a child, water running through the dirt at my feet?"

The stream from the front entrance at the Valentine garden finally sails through the tan gravel plain to a pair of platform benches and a carmine bougainvillea in full sunlight. The side garden ends here at the grand patio at the back of the house. Bright sunlight bounces off the house walls and across the concrete patio. I step over the threshold onto the patio, reluctantly leaving the journey of the stream.

EXPLORATIVE LINES

The grand patio at the Valentine garden functions as architectural space. It provides room for entertaining fifty or more guests against a view of the Pacific Ocean. Residents of Montecito and Santa Barbara, where quite a number of Greene's approximately five hundred private gardens are, generally prize the ocean views, but not so Greene—she refers to the ocean as the "dull blue thing out there." The water

Isabelle Greene, Valentine garden, rear terraces
Santa Barbara

is distant, not intimate the way Greene likes water; it does not unlatch time the way her stream does. Here on the patio, my alertness to the hillside oaks and the stream-scape fades, and I cross back into ordinary time. If I were walking with someone, this is the moment I would strike up conversation. The aura of the architecture and the ocean holds until the main garden comes into view.

The main garden appears first as an aerial view. It sits fifteen feet below the patio and descends in terraces down the hillside. But from the patio, it reads as a flat plane, and what is drawn there in the lines of the retaining walls and drifts of vegetation is a vast space. The garden expands so much in the mind, visitors have likened it to ancient rice terraces in Southeast Asia and to "a collision of continents."[5] There, picking its way across the fields, runs the familiar stream from the side garden, as if it had followed the bougainvillea, which spills from the patio over the wall.

Greene's lines were not always so imaginative or playful. Initially, her drawing, although well-executed, gained her no praise in Michael Dvortsak's Beginning Drawing class at UCSB in the late 1960s. She studied with Dvortsak for five or six years and credits those classes for giving her the courage to create landscapes as an artist.

Isabelle Haller (Greene),
Pinus jeffreyi cone,
pen and ink on paper, c. 1961

I had had this small career in botanical illustration. I'd gotten very precise and careful to render things just exactly the way they were. After a couple of weeks, the teacher stopped in the middle of the room, and he said, "I realize what I do. I walk around the room and if what you are doing really says something, I stop and talk with you, and if it doesn't, I pass you by." Well, it was real clear as the weeks went by that he had nothing to talk to me about. Then finally one day he did stop, and he said, "Isabelle, you're just too damn good for your own good. I am going to make you draw with your left hand." I was quite shattered, and I cried right then, in class, and I picked up the pen with my left hand and right off I made the most exquisite drawing you could imagine. The hand didn't know how to do it, and the mind was all turned upside down. I put my whole heart into it instead of my brain, and it turned out.[6]

Isabelle Haller (Greene), *Male Nude,*
charcoal on paper, c. 1966

Greene drew with her left hand for two years until she felt comfortable finding her way forward without ideas. That approach to art is also Greene's approach to landscape architecture. She calls it "leaping into nothingness."

At the beginning of a new project, Greene visits the site for many hours until it affects her. She is set to create a garden that encompasses more than beauty. Something bigger is always at stake:

> *Restoring a space to what it ought to be, something like that. Finding out where it was headed and helping it get there.*

She speaks similarly of drawing:

> *My lines explore their way into space. They are trying to find something—something right at the edge of my knowing that I can get to if I am really alive about that line.*

Isabelle Greene, Valentine garden rock signature, Santa Barbara

You can see Greene's process of bringing her landscapes brilliantly alive and into the realm of art by studying her landscape plans. She draws and redraws lines on layer upon layer of tissue paper, never erasing, just as Dvortsak taught her. She takes the plan to the site and, as she sculpts the land, which constitutes another exploration, reworks the lines into topography. Some of Greene's gardens—the ones with sufficient funding and collaboration from the clients to allow her to finish them to her satisfaction—earn her discreetly placed "IG" logo; at the Valentine garden the logo can be seen on a stone in the lower terrace of the main garden.

The stream at the Valentine garden illustrates a distinctly Greene line. In its vitality and progression across the garden, it mirrors dry washes meandering through the southern California landscape. In Greene's work, you can find many lines that evoke the natural formations of rock and water in the region. The trueness of the reproduction triggers an experience of the wild, even in a small garden; no other landscape architect recreates the wild landscape as well as Greene. The lines of the terrace fields at the Valentine garden call up a different landscape, however—one heavily marked by human intervention. It is the landscape in California's agricultural valleys, where the lines of crops and roads press hard on the geography, proceeding straight across the earth except where they are truncated by the curves of a river or a marsh. Greene photographs those agricultural/natural landscapes from airplanes; they mesmerize her.

I see in those photographs the contemporary state of landscape, human domination of nature side-by-side with a little bit of nature left to its own devices. In the Valentine garden, more clearly than in any of her other gardens, I imagine Greene confronting the modern crisis of landscape, our physical and spiritual alienation from the land, the lifeless duality in our thinking of land "as either an exploitable resource or as merely a scenic phenomenon."[7] She takes an agricultural model and has the landscape spring itself free, announcing its wildness in the most extraordinary way. The insistently geometric lines of the architecture of the Valentine residence may have pushed her to such a powerful articulation. Greene's distaste for geometric lines is almost an ethical one: she once said of the lines of the Valentine residence, they "try to pull away from nature, rise above and be free from it—and that's what's caused all this calamity in the world."

Isabelle Greene, Valentine garden, rear terrace retaining walls, Santa Barbara

The Valentine garden was the most difficult project in her career, Greene says, and she has never been so challenged since. In deference to the geometry of the residence, which she felt bound to respect, she built a wide, straight path through the terraces to align with the lower-floor entrance. The terrace walls are concrete, but Greene colored the concrete with a warm adobe hue and poured it into formwork made with cedar shakes, so that the texture of the wood appears on the face of the walls. She swung the lines of the walls across the garden in such a way that they seem to follow natural contours. The lines vibrate with a determined clarity; they have the "force of movement" that eighteenth-century artist Shen Tsung-ch'ien says "brings out the life of things."[8] Many years ago, I found a photograph of these terraces in a magazine; it was the first work I had seen of Greene's, and I felt the significance of it through the agitation in my body. I uttered my approval out loud. I knew I must one day stand on those terraces. I was "stirred"—in the way Greene uses the term to describe her experience of paradise.

The lines of these terraces manifest the life-force that we find in wild nature (and art—Tsung-ch'ien believed the force of movement in creative work came from the same source as the life-force in "the undulations of hilltops and every rock and tree"[9]). Yet Greene's terrace lines are not naturalistic, in the fashion of the stream. They bend away from nature toward abstraction. The effect of that makes the terraces magnificent in a second way. Not only do they effervesce with life, but they

Isabelle Greene, Valentine garden, rear terraces under construction, Santa Barbara

communicate with the architectural geometry, and a grand, joyous, right relationship arises between the house and Greene's continents of burgeoning plant life. Greene has done here what landscape architect Garrett Eckbo, in the late 1930s, insisted must be done. She has put "man and nature back together again."[10] A giddy harmony breaks out over this contemporary scene. Greene's lines resurrect hope. She rehabilitates land until it is fresh and there is no more dominion.

REVELATORY VIEWS

The aerial view presents an exhilarating way of seeing and inspires a sense of power. Le Corbusier was fascinated by the bird's eye view of earth: "the eye now sees in substance what the mind could only subjectively conceive," he wrote in the early 1930s. "It is a new source of measurement; it is the basis of a new sensation." He predicted it would change the world: "Man will make use of it to conceive new aims. Cities will arise out of their ashes."[11] The aerial view reveals afresh "an organic interdependency between humans and the natural world," writes James Corner.[12] It encouraged some modernist artists, including Le Corbusier, to launch a heroic new search for a universal order. The concentration on revealing an underlying order and "the dynamic and interactive connectedness between human life and the natural environment"[13] appears in Greene's work—in her commitment to land management and city planning as well as in her landscape architecture.

In every project, Greene aims to take down, at least metaphorically, garden boundaries and any impediments that might stall the eye or obstruct connection to the larger world. What she seeks, she says, is wholeness.

> *I will modulate the grading so you can see out or over or through; or shorten a hill or raise a flat area or carve away a downslope so you can see something. I'm always trying to go after the wholeness of things, because it's the big joining that's so important. A little patch of something, a garden, isn't very much unto itself. I like to see the rest, the big picture, and feel a part of it. I don't like enclosure; I don't like separation. Probably my attitude comes from tromping in the big landscape of the West... the big views and big terrain. I like things to join and to believe that they can be joined.*

Nothing on the terrace fields in the Valentine garden—not a vertical element or plant out of scale—interrupts the journey of the eye over the land. The eye runs free. So it is in many other of her gardens, but Greene has never truly decided whether she has finished the Valentine garden:

> *What's missing in it is some strong vertical, like a totem pole. When I'm standing up on the second floor, on the patio, I want to see something at eye level that starts down there and comes up to me.*

But if she made a permanent vertical element, such as the pole, it would surely ground the viewer in the garden and undermine the sense of a vast space. It would serve as a landmark, "giving a center to a fragment of the world," as architect Charles W. Moore explains in a discussion of landmarks and their role in landscape. As an example of the meaning of a landmark, Moore quotes Proust's recollections of the steeple at Combray:

There was a spot where the narrow road emerged suddenly on to an immense plain, closed at the horizon by strips of forest over which rose the fine point of Saint-Hilaire's steeple, but so sharpened and so pink that it seemed to be no more than sketched on the sky by the fingernail of a painter anxious to give to such a landscape, to so pure a piece of "nature," this little sign of art, this single indication of human existence.[14]

Greene avoids landmarks and "little signs of art," perhaps exactly because they would establish a human center in the wildness she conjures. More conventional landscape architects place a statue or arbor or some other "focal point" at the end of a vista, but Greene dislikes objects that catch the eye in a view. Rarely does she introduce any large solid upright or volume to a landscape, unless, for example, a wall is necessary to retain a slope. Greene works primarily on the horizontal, sculpting the lay of the land, sticking "at the bottom of the air space," as she puts it, clearing the way through to a view. To date the Valentine garden has no pole, so, with Greene's blessings, we may project ourselves out of it and away over the hillside oaks or into reverie.

UNABASHED BEAUTY

To descend the steps from the grand patio and walk into the main garden is to cross into bounty. The sunlight sparkles on the familiar slate shards, a delta of water brought to this dry land (one of the design challenges of the garden was its very small allotment of city water), and the softly textured plantings show Greene's signature play upon play of gray and green. The beauty has a special quality, of the type Elaine Scarry describes:

At the moment one comes into the presence of something beautiful, it greets you. It lifts away from the neutral background as though coming forward to welcome you.... It is as though the welcoming thing has entered into, and consented to, your being in its midst. Your arrival seems contractual, not just something you want, but something the world you are now joining wants.[15]

Greene finds such beauty in the Santa Ynez foothills. Describing a large landscape after a storm, the sky dark and low, slanting sunlight illuminating the foreground, she uses words similar to Scarry's:

It cancels everything I'm thinking, like I'm a child with no program, just giving myself to it—or it gives itself to me. In that instant, it's like a complete joining, like being in the eternal, primeval, primordial world. I feel I belong at the most fundamental level.

Being so enchanted, physically and spiritually, by nature did not find much of a place in mid- and late-twentieth-century art. For example, Piet Mondrian was as likely affected as Greene was by nature, but he sought to avoid it, insisting, his friends said, on changing seats if his had an outdoor view. Nature in the raw distracted him from expressing nature's repose through geometric planes and "the harmony of relations."[16] Natural beauty in all its regenerative power has been off-limits in the art world for a half century, says Patterson Sims. Instead, art focused on "the expanded centrality of the city and industry." But Sims believes the subject of nature has since been resurrected. Many contemporary artists are reconnecting with the natural world, some identifying themselves with the environmental movement. Sims says such work is "not idiosyncratic, marginalized, or out of sync, but normative, and today, ever more vitally necessary."[17]

Isabelle Greene, Valentine garden, rear terraces, view towards pergola, Santa Barbara

Before I leave the Valentine garden, I walk to the lowest corner of the garden, where Greene would have stood at the start of this project—she always walks away from the house to the farthest point of the garden to work out the long views. From here, my eye follows a rhythm of forms—from a carpet of hen-and-chicks rosettes to a silver-sworded yucca, past brilliant red roses waving from small pillars on the path to the flouncing red bougainvillea having the last laugh on the towering white wall.

The last laugh, did I write? Yes. Greene's work addresses design and environmental issues with great seriousness, but her resolutions are light with play. She admits she likes to "play with people's perception and their imagination, and get them into the game." ("Game?" I asked her. "You might say I leave little clues around," she replied. "It's an invitation into my mind—into what the garden has to offer that you haven't thought about.")

Those "clues" Greene strews about her gardens can draw one into an experience of paradise. Two years ago, she opened a public lecture with these words:

> *I came here tonight to explore paradise with you. I mean that paradise deep in the recesses of our minds—that place barely remembered and deeply internal, the sense that belongs to children—where we and the world were one thing.*

She talked of the paradise of the wild landscape and the paradise we seek by creating new artifacts—and the conflict between the two. Greene's mission as a landscape architect has always been to use her artist's skills and sensibilities to undo that conflict.

> *Each one of us helps either to bring the paradise to hand or to help it recede. Each of us starts from a particular place of heart and can adjust our path at any given time toward a better world where we humans can be at ease with each other and at one with a world that operates in a way that it will last.*

Isabelle Greene with Andy Neumann, Architect, Overall residence and garden under construction, Santa Barbara

POSTSCRIPT

Greene and I are sitting in a recently finished garden, at the Overall residence. The house, designed by architect Andy Neumann, rests against the steep Montecito hillside, melds with it, without separation. Greene comments that her grandfather, whose photograph hangs above her drafting table, built a house into a hillside in this way. She does not believe her work has been influenced by her grandfather's, but she describes him warmly as someone who built houses that were beautiful for his clients to live in, and she devotes herself similarly to her clients.

Isabelle Greene with Andy Neumann, Architect, Overall garden swimming pool, Santa Barbara

The terrace we are sitting on allows Mr. Overall to step comfortably from the house down to the pool, which lies in front of us. The "greeting" beauty that drives Greene's reputation surrounds us. Nothing has changed in her approach to landscape architecture since the Valentine garden or even since her first, award-winning, landscape project forty years ago. She continues to build gardens that are stirringly beautiful and "whole." Greene seems pleased, and not just with the lay of the land or the ways she has darned the site to the hillside. Observing her work in the Overall garden, she speaks excitedly about the strong lines she introduced. She is thrilled by the tall concrete retaining walls that were needed to hold the soil around the mature oaks on the site. They cross the hillside in bold, dramatic arcs, the ends of each wall tapering into the slope. She eyes with satisfaction the pool edge, which sits on the front of the terrace, like the wall of a dam. Its strong and graceful line—much more abstract than natural—converses with Neumann's lyrical minimalism.

> This was my way of being like Andy Neumann—taking a line, giving it ease, and making it pure, with no distortions of the idea. Was I aching to be purer, simpler when I was building this? My inclinations have always been organic, rustic, textural—here I was lunging out for the other. It's been satisfying.

Greene once expressed fear that pursuing purity might mean intellectual separation from her beloved natural world. Jane Howarth writes about the "fine line between...developing nature's own aesthetic potential and imposing a design on it which might have the effect of incorporating it into the world of art and artifact."[18] Greene's work transcends those two choices.

Much depends, Greene thinks, on the quality of her lines (Matisse, committed also to expressing paradise, said, "My line drawing is the purest and most direct translation of my emotion"[19]). As her landscape architecture practice has grown, taking her all over the country, her time available for drawing has decreased. She intends to commit more time to drawing. Her energy rises at the prospect of it.

Out of habit, I think, but still with evident pleasure, she comments on the floating horizontality of the terrace levels before us and the drop in height of the old oaks from uphill to downhill, like the natural fall of the land. But she holds her gaze longest on her strongest lines.

Isabelle Greene painting at the Duca residence, Carpinteria, 1997

NOTES

[1] Elizabeth B. Kassler, *Modern Gardens and the Landscape* (New York: The Museum of Modern Art, 1964), 8.

[2] All quotations of Isabelle Greene are from conversations with the author unless otherwise noted.

[3] Susan Stewart, *On Longing: Narratives of the Miniature, the Gigantic, the Souvenir, the Collection* (Durham, NC: Duke University Press, 1993), 67.

[4] Jane Brown, *The Modern Garden* (New York: Princeton Architectural Press, 2000), 60.

[5] See Nancy Goslee Power, Susan Heeger, Mick Hales, *The Gardens of California: Four Centuries of Design from Mission to Modern* (New York: C. Potter, 1995), 171.

[6] Some of Isabelle Greene's botanical illustrations are in the permanent collection of the Hunt Botanical Library in Pittsburgh, Pennsylvania.

[7] James Corner and Alex S. MacLean, in their introduction to *Taking Measures Across the American Landscape* (New Haven: Yale University Press, 1996), xix.

[8] Shen Tsung-ch'ien, as quoted in Martin Gayford and Karen Wright, eds., *The Grove Book of Art Writing* (New York: Grove Press, 1998), 48.

[9] Ibid., 47.

[10] Garrett Eckbo, as quoted in Peter Walker and Melanie Louise Simo, *Invisible Gardens: The Search for Modernism in the American Landscape* (Cambridge: MIT Press, 1994), 123.

[11] Le Corbusier, as quoted in Corner and MacLean, *Taking Measures Across the American Landscape*, 15.

[12] Ibid.

[13] Ibid., xix.

[14] Marcel Proust, as quoted in Charles W. Moore, William J. Mitchell, William Turnbull, *The Poetics of Gardens* (Cambridge: MIT Press, 1988), 30.

[15] Elaine Scarry, *On Beauty and Being Just* (Princeton: Princeton University Press, 1999), 25-26.

[16] Piet Mondrian, as quoted in Brown, *The Modern Garden*, 19.

[17] Patterson Sims, "Resurrecting Nature," *Orion* 23 (March/April 2004): 36.

[18] Jane Howarth, "A Railway Runs through It," in Vicki Berger and Isabel Vasseur, *Arcadia Revisited: The Place of Landscape* (London: Black Dog Publishing, 1997), 143.

[19] Henri Matisse, "Notes of a Painter on His Drawing," in Gayford and Wright, *The Grove Book of Art Writing*, 412.

Isabelle Greene, Silver Garden, Longwood Gardens, Kennett Square, Pennsylvania

PLACE IN DESIGN: An Interview with Isabelle Greene

Kurt G.F. Helfrich
Curator, Architecture and Design Collection
University Art Museum
University of California, Santa Barbara

The following interview was conducted at the office of Isabelle C. Greene and Associates in Santa Barbara, California on October 26, 2004, when installation plans for the exhibition *Isabelle Greene: Shaping Place in the Landscape* were well underway.

Kurt Helfrich: Isabelle, today I want to talk about the dry-scape installation that you are creating as part of the upcoming exhibition of your work, *Isabelle Greene: Shaping Place in the Landscape*, at the University Art Museum, University of California, Santa Barbara in the spring of 2005. I would also like to talk about some larger issues that may have inspired it—in particular the issue of sustainability.

In developing the exhibition plan, we were challenged by the idea of bringing a garden to a museum—of finding a means to showcase the artistry behind how you shape the environment to create a sense of place. I think your installation addresses this issue extremely effectively. Please discuss some of the key elements behind your dry-scape installation strategy.

Isabelle Greene: I think what I am doing in bringing the garden—or, you might say, the land—into the museum is exploding the museum and taking it to the outdoors. If anything I am saying to people, "do not rush indoors; stay outdoors and look around, look at what is there, hang on to it!" That is something I always want people to do—I want people to listen, to take in…and listen…as if to themselves.

I believe that most of the time, most people are actually shut off from themselves; that is why they make big mistakes, like spoiling the earth and using up resources. If you have any sensitivity about you at all, you know that dirty water is horrible. You know that murky skies are unpleasant; you know that sitting on hot pavement is uncomfortable. But, at least in America, especially in urban America, people are trained from the time they are toddlers to sort of deny those feelings and get straight-laced about the world. This is too big an issue for discussing right now, but the point is, I want people, when they get their first view of the installation, to go, "Oh, wow!" and to somehow grasp this heart of life, this earth—to pause, and take it in—and feel something profound, like I am now, just talking about it.

KH: From the viewers' perspective, they are going to arrive at the Museum to find a marker leading them in—a boulder you are selecting for the Museum plaza.

IG: I will call it a "calling card." I think it is going to intrigue them, to call them inside. I think it is going to be a surprise. Actually, I want this whole exhibition to be a surprise. I want people to find themselves viewing something they did not expect to see, and seeing things they have never seen before. And they will have some sensations about it, I hope. I myself take such delight in the earth's forms and the mysterious shreds of clouds, and the nubbery of our mountains' clothing (the chaparral). I have this far-out idea that I can bring that delight to the people viewing this exhibit for the first time.

KH: That stone, that calling card, as you say, will lead people into the Museum, where they will enter the Nachman Courtyard Gallery and find more stones. What are your thoughts about what they will see there?

IG: What we have there is a sense of tall things—something you do not expect in an art gallery. Some of them are craggy and belong in the outdoors—just inevitably *outdoors* things, right there in the sunlight of the atrium. There are also some gauzy things that you can see right through and do not seem to belong anywhere in this world. People are going to have to begin fighting to make sense of that. Some will have a lot of trouble with it.

KH: Yes they will, but this is why I think it is so marvelous. This show, which is so much more than a traditional retrospective, is not just a presentation of your work from the past. It is what happens when you have a designer working *with* a museum—

IG: —while she is exploring herself...in exploring the design of the landscape. You and I are on this little trip, and we don't know where it's going.

KH: I think you know where you are going. You have envisioned a large aperture connecting the Nachman Courtyard Gallery and the Main Gallery that allows a person to look straight ahead toward an incredible, abstracted, mountain landscape. What is amazing to me is that here, with this one image, you have presented the essence of what matters in your work—what has helped you create based on place, and based on what you know—

IG: —what I know and what I *love*—

KH: —which are the mountains and foothills of Santa Barbara. Have you considered other ecological forms as well?

IG: I have thought of doing something the way the desert is. The desert is pure earth; there is nothing covering up the forms. There is nothing clogging up the view and obscuring things. And desert spaces are huge and vast. In a way I got a little bit of that into my cactus installation in the greenhouse of the Longwood garden in Pennsylvania. The floor plane of the desert is clear and clean, and against it you can see the absolutely straight lines of the alluvial fans and how they

Isabelle Greene, *Mountains*, charcoal on paper, n.d.

come for miles out of the mountains…. So, yes, I would love to work with that somewhere.

But this project is about *our* mountains. I learned to love mountains and streams and boulders and all that happens with them in Pasadena, where I grew up, but Pasadena's mountains are a lot steeper and more sterile than ours: kind of nubby and drier. Our mountains, being as close to the ocean as they are, have very lush chaparral, not sparse—very lush, completely happy chaparral.

Isabelle Greene, *Mountains near San Luis Obispo*, watercolor on paper, 1986

Actually, there are some places in the Santa Monica mountains where there is what I love here—but not in the San Gabriel mountains. In the Santa Monica mountains, the disjunction between soils creates a really clean line between where the grasslands stop and the chaparral begins. It goes up and down, over ridges and in valleys, but always there is this line—it is golden against green, and it is soft and fuzzy.

KH: After viewers get a glimpse of this landscape, they then go into a section that presents your career and aspects of a number of your gardens. We talked about ending this section with a presentation of your most recent work, for the Santa Barbara Natural History Museum. You mentioned to me earlier that some of the things you are dealing with right now—in relation to the Natural History Museum's creek restoration project and even their master planning project—grow out of and reinforce your interest in Santa Barbara's foothills and mountains. Indeed, what resonates greatly through all of this is how your career here has used the mountains and the foothills as a backdrop in one way or another.

IG: More as a presence than a backdrop. There are, however, some gardens that do not relate to the mountains at all. In particular, I am thinking of the Lovelace garden. It is green, green, green; it is an English-style house and there are English-style borders and I love that. And there is this little nooky pool under the canopy of the oaks, so that you feel very intimate (it almost is a space unto itself). Although, actually, there are places where you can view the lawn, and the house, with the mountains beyond—so, there you are. But the mountains do not play a big part.

KH: Do the mountains have anything to do with the abstract form of the pool in the Lovelace garden, like the abstraction you are playing with for the installation?

IG: No, I do not think so. But the boulders in the installation come from my childhood memories of ravines, which relate to the crevices that water makes, running down the mountains.

KH: Is that a fantasy fulfilled for you—a fulfillment of something you treasured as a child, from being in those kinds of rock formations? Are you creating a stable environment that will allow you to put yourself within the space of those boulders safely?

IG: I do not think "safely" is a part of it—but playing with the boulders and playing with water is. For the Singing Spring job, there was quite a bit of property and the owner, bless his heart, wanted overland drainage rather than drainage piping, which meant that by the time all of the water went from one edge of the property to the other, the little "gullies," or "rivulets," were fairly deep. When we got through setting all the rocks and creating the drainage channels and the fine grading was done, it was like a beautiful monochromatic mini-landscape. It was very sensuous, and I remember standing there with my boots on (I used to wear boots just to walk around in the dust, by the way) and a dress and a hat, sweating. It was so hot I could hardly stand it. When they turned on the sprinklers to test them further up, a little rivulet of water came meandering its way down the crease of the swale and

trickled between my boots (I was straddling the "ravine")—this little spit of water sparkling its way through the sunshine…. I remembered as a child playing in the mud and water behind my grandmother's house in the summer.

KH: How does that extend in terms of what you are doing for the Mission Creek restoration project for the Natural History Museum?

Isabelle McElwain (Greene) on a family camping trip, 1936

IG: Of course, that is a very responsible thing, isn't it?—not too much like playing in the mud. On the other hand, it is more like playing God in a way.

KH: Are you comfortable with that?

IG: Oh, yes. Yes, very. Let's eliminate these buildings—they do not look good and they harm the watershed—and let's take up the paving—because it would be nice to have vegetation—and let's recreate the parking with groundcovers and cement wheel-tracks, like they used to have for driveways, instead of all this sea of paving, and so on. It is a lot of engineering, a lot of careful, careful engineering, manipulating grades with a slide rule and a calculator, observing percentages and codes… altogether very adult, responsible things. But it is still delicious—because it is returning things at least to a natural functioning, even if not a natural look.

KH: One meaning of the word restoration is to return something to the state it was in before. Do you believe that is possible—that we can even know what that was?

IG: No, I don't. Did you know, it has been discovered that as far back as anyone knows, the natives of America always managed their forests and grasslands, and even chaparral and deserts, by burning? So who knows when that did not happen? It is so far back, it is sort of irrelevant. I have moved from wanting to manipulate things to *look* a certain way, to wanting to manipulate things so they *function* a certain way—so they function joyfully.

KH: Can you give me an example of how you are doing this with your work for the Santa Barbara Natural History Museum?

IG: Yes, I'm doing many, many things that relate to function. And by the way, those cement tracks are not so much a return to nature—although they do make the landscape grassier and lovelier—but a return to older times, which I draw on all the time. It is comforting, I think, for people to recall and bring forward things that were part of their upbringing, or their parents' upbringing, or their grandparents'.

KH: You are using more natural material, but it is still human intervention—and you do not deny that, which I think is important.

IG: Oh, no denial. We would have to kill off all the humans to get rid of all human intervention! It was on the Petersen and Overall projects—about seven jobs back—when I first realized that I wanted to have water go as it wanted, naturally. I remember on the Petersen job being sort of baffled by the lot lying downgrade. The drainage historically sheeted off of the southwest corner, where there was a nice little place where the water gathered. It was a little boggy, and it went under the fence to the neighbor's property. Then, because we put gutters on the roof and an underground drainage system on the north side of the house to save the foundations and floors and walls, we had more water. Legally, you cannot change drainage across property lines, so we were not allowed to let it flow to that nice little boggy place. I forget exactly what we did: we put in a pipe someplace and a drain, and off it went.

Isabelle Greene with Andy Neumann, Architect, Overall garden courtyard, Santa Barbara

I remember being frustrated because I couldn't arrange this water flow as it wanted to go.

The water, you know, wants to land on the mountains and the hills and everything, and sheet down into the little ravines and collect, and be a stream and scour the boulders and get down to the ocean like it always has. But when that cannot happen, it seems like some kind of abortion. On the Overall job, I made a concerted effort from the very beginning to try to let the water penetrate soils and not be collected into pipes. Again it was difficult: it was a pretty steep site and there was considerable chance for cave-ins. I ended up with lots of area drains and other things, but we managed to let much of it fall naturally and flow into two ravines on either side of the house.

Now, with the Santa Barbara Natural History Museum, we have a much easier site to deal with, because it is not so steep, and I get my heart's dream: to take out all the gruesome hard paving, eliminate all the pipes (those nasty little holes in the ground), and return everything to functioning watercourses, with living plants in them. Let the plants do their work of cleansing the water, and let the water be on the surface, finding its way across the low places I have made for it, and finally into the creek, like it should—then it is property that is functioning the way it should, and that, you know, is a joy!

KH: This is perfect, Isabelle, because I want to go back to the dry-scape installation for the Museum, and I want you to talk about the water element that you are thinking about abstracting for the section on your work for the Santa Barbara Natural History Museum.

IG: I would like every person in Santa Barbara to have a map of their watershed in their head, so they respect the fact that it does not just start at the faucet and then end at the sewer drain. This is my method: the main entry plaza at the Museum will have an accurate representation of our creeks and rivulets right in the pavement, so you cannot get into the Museum without walking on your watershed.

KH: The watershed here goes from the top of the mountain all the way down?

IG: From the very ridge top. By the way, I think watershed is secondary—my first love is the mountains themselves. But the water makes little courses in them as it finds its way down and makes those wonderful shapes.

KH: So, in a way, this is a new, but completely related, interest.

IG: Definitely my interest in how water functions is new, but I have always loved getting intimate with water. All my life, if I found a puddle I would get in it. And when I was growing up, if I found a lake or a pond I would throw off my clothes and go swim in it. I swam in the ocean daily. But the ocean is not interesting in the way the watershed is: it is not as immediate, tactile, or sensuous.

KH: When you designed that beautiful ledge in the Larkin garden, the deck area that goes out to the ocean, how did you use the ocean in your design?

IG: The deck reflected wave action, the way the end of the wave that sweeps up the beach leaves thin lines—intersecting arcs with a little ridge of foam around them. I was thinking of that. But I was also thinking about the sea wall, with its strong, prominent, masonry shape: I just had to relate to that shape. It was the strongest pattern….

KH: Your love of water—is that something you think is unique to the fact that you are from California, as it is such a scarce resource here? And how does that fit in with your design work, and the appeal of lushness, and your love also of the desert?

IG: Ever since I was a child I loved the iridescence of water and the sparkle of it—the reflection, and the way grains of sand inside work with it. There is something aesthetically exquisite about water… especially in the sunshine. But I fight with that inside myself. I struggle with it. I am apt to be critical of people who come here from other, wetter places and want to behave exactly as they did in the places they came from. I feel if you want to be here, you must learn *how* to be here.

KH: But is that not a part of the whole history of landscape design here—people coming and wanting to create the image of what they knew before?

IG: Yes, it is, and you cannot stop it. You can try, but you cannot stop it. So, for instance, in regards to lawns, I always encourage people to shrink the amount of lawn, and I get away with that a lot of the time; there are some clients who are happy with no lawn whatsoever. But lawn does have a pretty, green color. It is even and smooth, and you can walk on it—it is sympathetic; you can use it for human purposes. I notice that even I respond sometimes to pretty, green colors and to the simplicity of a lawn. There is almost nothing else that provides such a restful element, such simplicity—except maybe a sheet of water.

Isabelle Haller (Greene), Santa Barbara Psychiatric Clinic front lawn, Santa Barbara

KH: So there is a part of you that likes lawns?

IG: It is not productive to like lawns, because it fights our limitations. But I think there is a kind of instinctual thing in all humans to long for water—the looks of water, the use of water, the luxuriousness and the abundance of water—and just to want it around. But when I am in the desert, I do not have that longing for water. And if I see somebody's lawn lying uneasily out there in the desert, like a little patch of green hair…. It is just so…*unfitting.*

KH: The ecosystem here in Santa Barbara is very rich and interesting—a mixture of dry and wet conditions. It is dry, but the ocean humidifies year-round through the marine layer, and that provides a kind of lushness, as you mentioned earlier, to the chaparral which does not exist elsewhere. Still, it is not a lushness that you might have in places where it rains or is moist all year.

IG: Nothing like it at all. As a matter of fact, I try to steel myself for it, and try to embrace it, when the long summer gets more and more tired. The chaparral up there—which is seasonally so beautiful—loses its green color and begins to brown. It gets brittle, and the individual leaves curl up, and a lot of them just fall off—only twigs remain…. That is also the fire season, which is really scary.

Nevertheless, there are still a few plants that keep sprouting up through the endless summer that provide some interest. *Gnaphalium*, or Pearly Everlasting, comes up somehow in this dry soil; it is ghostlike silver, which I love. And the old *Rhumex* has its rusty stalks that provide nice contrast with the *Toyons* coming right up through it, in fine shape, doing their flowers followed by their little red berries—a show stopper. And, once in a while, we get a summer rain—it smells so good, and is exciting!

Still, an awful lot is just hanging on, waiting for the rain. The dry, standing weeds, which are so golden and beautiful in June and July, begin to lose their waxen color and actually get some kind of sticky, gummy marine air clinging to them, with little bits of molds, and dirt, and so on. They get kind of brown, and then they go on and get grayish, and then they break apart, brittle, flagging in the season's hottest weather, coated with dust…. It's pretty tough. I think autumn is perhaps the hardest season to understand and to love. Not only are we without rain, we may have gone without it for a long time.

However, in a funny way, I even like that hard difficulty, just like I want hard jobs that make me sweat and roll up my sleeves and get intimate with the work, and engage and put everything into fighting back....

KH: Yes. That is the way you work and that is the way you design, which leads me to my next question. What role does your interest in sustainability play into the installation?

IG: "Sustainability" is a word that is running around now. Thank God—if everybody knows what it means, then it is going to bring some good. But, basically, doesn't it just mean things working well together—properly, in wholeness? How can anybody escape going to that, how could anybody not want that? But, you know, I did not consider using this exhibit to tell the story of recycling and sustainable practices. This exhibit, actually, is not much of a "green" exhibit. For me, that is the least interesting point—all that does is act like frosting on the cake. This exhibit is just to put out an appeal for people to love something, in the hopes that that will draw them to the bigger picture—the greater systems and functions of this earth.

KH: For me, the brilliance about the exhibit is that you are trying very directly to get people to treasure what is probably the single most noticeable thing in their landscape: these mountains and foothills.

IG: Exactly—to get people to treasure them.

KH: And what is interesting is that your work has been about doing that pretty much from the very beginning.

IG: Absolutely.

KH: Also in the exhibit you have included the notion of cladding the chiseled Styrofoam mountain in the Main Gallery with different materials—with human hair, wood chips, or floating steel wool pads. Let me ask you, why the human hair? What is your thinking about that?

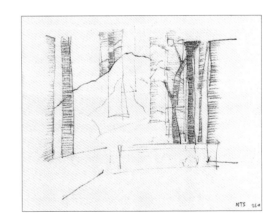

Isabelle Greene, University Art Museum exhibition Main Gallery dry-scape installation (proposed), *View into Gallery Showing Mountain and Banners,* graphite on vellum, Santa Barbara, 2004

IG: Grasses are so luminous in the early and middle part of summer, when they are still standing fresh, freshly dried. They are luminous and waxen gold, with a quality that I would love to capture in paint or something. And they are so silky, those hills—such sensuous forms covered with a silky light. I wanted to try to capture that effect using anything that speaks to that at all. The only thing I could think of was golden blond human hair, and the way it catches light. It has the right colors. With grasses, the space around each stalk goes clear down to the ground, so around each stalk there is light, I guess, that goes all the way down to the ground as well—you sense that when you see a stand of grass. Then the slightest ripple of breeze moves the whole business, and you see waves going across the hills....

Isabelle Greene, University Art Museum exhibition Main Gallery dry-scape installation (proposed), *View of Rear of Mountain*, graphite on vellum, Santa Barbara, 2004

KH: Steel wool would represent the clouds? Is that correct?

IG: Oh, that is a secondary notion—kind of a zany notion. First of all, the steel wool will represent the chaparral: the solid, articulate, dense, edge-to-edge chaparral covering the mountains. Then (but so as not to be too literal about this), I did envision the far edge of it not being quite graspable, like the edge of the exhibit—kind of peeling off of the form, lifting up and becoming cloudlike. Frankly, I have no idea how well that will come off. It is a big experiment. But, I can imagine getting steel wool pads up on sticks, or hung from wires, or whatever it's going to be. Then there is the experimenting with the coloration. Somehow we are going to have to transition from khaki to bluish white. That is the big question, transitioning....

KH: Isabelle, one of the things that strike me is the sense that in your life, your daily living patterns, you have brought things from the inside of you out—you have been able to make personal things sustainable, creating a whole from within that also shapes and informs your landscapes.

IG: I think of myself as this...this...experimentation mechanism. I have a span of life. It is mine. I have my body, my brains, and my eyes, and there really is no fixed or immutable structure beyond that. It is all about what I am willing to take on—what I am willing to "stomach," what I am willing to account for, what I am willing to do with it. This is sort of unusual—in fact, I have never heard anybody talk that way. You know, Gandhi decided to experiment with two things. He experimented with truth and with non-violence, and on as vast a scale as he was able. I like that—"as vast a scale."

It is interesting and illustrative for me—to decide on a path, or an attitude, or a commitment, and then watch myself to see what happens. I write my own ticket, so to speak, invent my own feedback mechanism. And I will deliberately make a commitment or take an attitude that is going to change me. I am aware I am going to have to give up something in the process. But, if I see a goal as being worth it, I just kind of let myself become whatever I need to be and watch it happen, because I *trust* the process. I think that is what is unusual: most people will try to hang on to who they are at the moment, but I am quite willing to change who I am in the service of a goal. Yes, from myself outward is how it goes. I am much less interested in going over *there* and manipulating *you*, because that is your job. My job stays with being about me.

KH: That's right. In a recent conversation, you mentioned how your creative work has taken on a series of new directions. Could you, as a conclusion, give me a few thoughts about what you see as

Isabelle Haller (Greene), Santa Barbara Psychiatric Clinic north patio, Santa Barbara

the differences between Isabelle Haller (as you were known previously) and Isabelle Greene (your mother's maiden name, by which you are now known)—the differences between you in 1964, when you had your first commission (for the Santa Barbara Psychiatric Clinic) and now, in 2004?

IG: That is a good question. First of all, I will tell you the things that are the same. On my very first job, at the Santa Barbara Psychiatric Clinic, I went through the same process as I do now, and I dealt with the same elements. For instance, I recycled material, and not out of any philosophy. When they took up the driveway, I said, "Can I have the pieces?," and then I made them into stepping stones, in a very Japanese, carefully, carefully arranged way. They were beautiful. I also arranged two very nice places for people to sit, each of which was thought out exactly: one is shady and utterly private; the other is sunlit and set at the public entrance, although it is still a little bit shielded. I worked on the bench height and step heights…. I did a bit of architectural commentary. I had something to say about color, plaster, the shape of walls, and other things.

KH: For that project you worked with Paul Tuttle, right?

IG: Yes, that was when we first crossed paths. I also dealt with circulation. I considered that pedestrians needed separation from the driveway, so I put in sidewalks. I dealt with the neighbors: I jogged the fence where a window was up against it. I placed boulders along the parking strip, done in decomposed granite rather than in lawns. I experimented with stray plants that I was unfamiliar with (which worked out). I used some colors; I referenced Burle Marx a bit. Today, too, I have architectural comment, but far more.

KH: Right. That has really taken off, hasn't it?

IG: Oh yes. First of all, in a nutshell, I am far more confident. I've always felt my way, every time— I want the chance to feel my way; I would get bored if I did the same old thing—but now I feel secure and happy in that. I don't worry about it.

KH: Does your confidence come from doing these things, and doing them right, as part of a greater whole?

IG: I think so. Getting my landscape architectural license changed things for me an awful lot. For the first time I knew what knowledge other people had, and I knew that my knowledge matched.

KH: How would you characterize your training as a landscape designer?

IG: Half of my career is self-trained. For the first five, ten, or fifteen years, I was afraid to look behind me at any of the jobs I had done. I felt like I was going to collapse—trees were going to die; clients were going to hate it. I was frightened to death. I did not think I had done anything at all. I felt I had not been there and put something there. I was just moving forward, trying to get away from what was there behind. It was strange. But in the last ten to fifteen years, I began to realize that some of those are wonderful gardens, clients enjoy the designs, the work is solid, and I have a lovely business building up.
        But I think the confidence has come from personal experimentation rather than just career experience. It comes from having made enough decisions on my own. "I will see what happens if I do this." Something does happen: I make an assessment that is correct, another one that is not. I decide I will do this next time, try that another time. And I have done that a million times, so I feel like I am standing on this mountain of experience that is mine. It did not come from anybody else, it is not in reference to anybody else, and it is not beholden to anybody else. Nothing can take it away from me. I know that. I think that is the confidence. And now I can step out into the darkness with perfect ease and happiness. Furthermore, I am willing to throw my life, my reputation, my career at it and go for broke, experimenting with things, trying things…. I still like to experiment with plants, just a few every job. I know an awful lot more about which plants are going to give you trouble than I used to; I stay away from them.

KH: But there is no way you can really know that unless you let them cycle through. That is the reality of landscape design. It is not like a building—

IG: —it is made up of moving parts—

KH: —and it continues to move. A building requires human intervention and has a moment when it is finished, but a landscape is dependent on the environment and continues to develop. Is that the difference, then, for you, between landscape design and architecture?

IG: Well, landscape is so vast. It is huge, and it is flexible and responsive. It is filled with organic things and living systems. It is so much more of a lively medium. I am so grateful I am in the landscape field. I have been pretty lucky: most of my clients leave their landscapes the way I left them. Some of them, heartrendingly, are still honoring the original design after thirty years. The Lovelaces recently wanted to add two Adirondack chairs at the end of the lawn. They commissioned every little thing as one would of an artist. I worked on that project for several months, getting the right chairs, the right size….

By now, fortunately, most of the clients who come to me know ahead of time what I have to offer; they come for that and they love that. I think it is because I have done the experiments right. I have said my piece. I never hold back and I have never waffled. I have never compromised myself. Therefore my outlines are clear, and you can pretty much tell who you are getting.

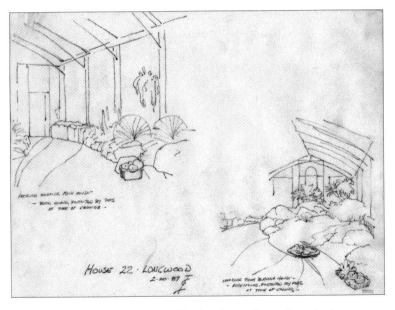

Isabelle Greene, Silver Garden, Longwood Gardens, Kennett Square, Pennsylvania, *Preliminary Interior Elevations*, graphite on vellum, 1987

KH: I have one last question for you. For your Longwood project, you worked in Pennsylvania, in a completely different environment. This allowed you to comment in the abstract on the climate and the landscape with which you are so intimately involved. Would you have any interest in designing a landscape for a client in, say, Michigan?

IG: I would be delighted. I am happy to move around. I don't like to be moving so frequently that jobs cannot be consistent and the office cannot be maintained—I really want the office to run smoothly and be in good control—so that would preclude running off to Florida or Mexico or Italy all the time,

Isabelle McElwain (Greene) in the desert, 1939

which some people do. But to have a really good client in Michigan, that would be good.

KH: David Streatfield once mentioned to me how sad it seems to him when landscape architects who do projects all over the world are so busy that they do not take the time to understand the specifics of a particular locale or context. This creates something completely inappropriate.

IG: A pastiche.

KH: I cannot see you doing that.

IG: Anyplace I would go I would want to nest there for a while—really soak it up, sop it up, get intimate with it. Then I would probably play off of how I saw it in a semi-abstract way. That is what I would like to believe I would do. Over the course of those many trips to Pennsylvania, I began to get a sensation of rocking hills, little rocking hills…. It was a kind of rhythm, and I longed to do something with that. I never did, but I still remember the sense of those little rounded landscapes.

Isabelle Greene at Antelope Valley, 1983

KH: How long would it take you to get a sense of a place? Would you need at least a full cycle of the different seasons?

IG: I do not think so. I do not think that is what I would be after. It would be the land forms, whatever they were…. As to plants, when I have done jobs in other parts of the country, such as in Florida and Alabama, I have gone to nurseries and browsed the plants that were for sale, and of course looked at the woods and the fields, and bought books. If it was a major job, I would work through the nurseries to find good, local contractors, and then just do the normal things: be as close to them as I could; bring some in and try them out; continue the process of exploring and experimenting. It is funny that I used to want to do a roof garden in New York. I also wanted to do a villa in France, and a couple of other things like that. But that has all been done; it is behind. I am really not compelled there.

KH: Even the roof garden in Manhattan?

IG: No. That too has been done. It is mechanical; everybody has been showing off things like that for a while—and it is old. But to go to some raw area in a new country like Australia and do something appropriate there—that would be very, very interesting. Or New Zealand, for instance, or any place in the west. I do not know for sure what I would do with prairie country, but it would be interesting. Woods country… I know I could do something there. And old farm country….

KH: In a conversation with David Streatfield, you mentioned how entranced you are when you fly over the country and look down and see landscapes in the largest sense—

IG: —yes, the patterns…the clues, and the messages—

KH: That interest of yours, to my mind, relates to your way of going to a place to soak it up— of trying to find the larger patterns shaping that particular place, and then playing off of those in an abstracted way.

IG: You understand me awfully well, Kurt. Thank you.

Isabelle Haller (Greene) at the top of Mount Langley, 1954

Isabelle Greene, Valentine garden, Santa Barbara

INES ROBERTS: Interpreting Isabelle Greene's Landscapes

Karen Sinsheimer
Curator of Photography
Santa Barbara Museum of Art

For one visual artist to both understand and interpret another artist's creation in an entirely different medium requires a particular sensibility. While searching for a photographer who could understand and interpret the landscapes of Isabelle Greene, I identified any number of great photographers, but I had to look no further than Santa Barbara to find a passionate, articulate observer of the world order who has lived here for several decades.

Ines Roberts moved to Santa Barbara in 1966, coincidentally the same year Isabelle Greene completed her first landscape design project. For the past four decades, Roberts not only has lived in and explored the Santa Barbara landscape with her camera, she also has roamed through far-flung parts of the world—when she has not been soaring above it in her hang glider, camera in tow. From the moment she took up photography, she was passionate about the medium. "I am fully aware," says Roberts, "that I am addicted to photography—that it is not only part of my life, but of my self...."[1]

Roberts's photography, acknowledged worldwide, is regularly published in Britain and Europe. A fellow of the Royal Photographic Society of Great Britain, she was invited by the London Salon of Photography to become a member in 1996. She had won several first-place medals in the Salon's annual competitions, but was unaware of how exclusive membership is: the group totals thirty-five worldwide and Ines Roberts was only the third woman inducted into membership in the club's 104-year history. In 2003, the *BBC Wildlife Magazine* and the Natural History Museum of London accorded her the title Wildlife Photographer of the Year, in the category of Wild Places.

In 2000, when work on the exhibition of Isabelle Greene's career had just begun, Isabelle Greene and Ines Roberts knew of each other, but their paths had yet to converge. When Greene viewed some of Roberts's initial images of her Valentine garden, she knew that a sympathetic match had been made. Both professionals work intuitively and each approaches a new project site in much the same way. The Santa Barbara Museum of Art commissioned Ines Roberts to create a photographic interpretation of five gardens designed by Greene; these images are exhibited in collaboration with the University of California, Santa Barbara's University Art Museum as part of their exhibition, *Isabelle Greene: Shaping Place in the Landscape.*

Roberts launched her visual journey of Greene's gardens in the year 2000 and never needed another cue. Always mindful of owners' privacy, she arranged visits to each garden, often for several hours at a time, to explore the different landscapes as the seasons and weather changed. Roberts noted, "Visiting five gardens over a period of four years, I expected a repetition of layout and similar impressions. It filled me with admiration when I discovered that each garden was different. They are designed not only to respect the owners' personalities and wishes, but also to incorporate the atmosphere of the surrounding landscape."

Ines Roberts' approach to subject matter has been honed over time. Whether photographing household items, manmade structures, or the pristine landscape, she seeks to reveal other realities—to uncover unseen connections, to discover hidden truths. Her interpretations range from representation to abstraction, which to her are not stylistically contradictory but, rather, differing expressions of the complex relationship between the object and the idea.

Roberts covets the solitude of exploration. "I am excited and overwhelmed by the dramatic moments in nature, but I am more in tune with contemplative settings and still moods...they are shyly inviting me to stay and look, and they make room for my own senses to unfold and celebrate. Isabelle Greene's landscapes instilled the impression of isolation and stillness, but with the reassuring charm of being invited." As the photographer spent time in the five gardens, she discovered the structures and rhythms of each garden that establish its unique connection to the natural world. At the same time, her images reveal the underlying themes and threads that both connect and distinguish Greene's landscapes.

Golden, natural rocks and boulders are found in each of the estates, but they are placed and arranged to emphasize the landscape, not to dominate or interrupt it. Roberts focused on the way in which rocks function as vessel or path, shade or enclosure. Every one of Greene's landscapes photographed by Roberts includes a swimming pool, though each differs profoundly in design. The photographer captured the essence of water, reflector and seductress. The arrangement of plants, water, concrete, and stone presented an ever-changing yet prevailing theme that Roberts explored in each site. Bare walls are transformed by graceful, flowering creepers or vines, which soften an otherwise austere space. "In all these gardens the native trees are allowed to go on growing. They become part of the new design."

Ines Roberts' photographs are subjective interpretations or translations of what she discovered. She understood that pure documentation would rob these landscapes of their spiritual atmosphere, and so she translated what she felt and saw and what was meaningful to her, while at the same time hoping to convey her admiration and delight in the landscapes of Isabelle Greene. Nevertheless, it remained a challenge for her to represent Greene's landscapes. As she succinctly summarized, "It is a little bit like holding a shell to a person's ear, who has never been at the sea, and hoping to convey the feeling of the ocean."

NOTES

[1] All quotations of Ines Roberts are from an unpublished artist's statement, October 2004.

Isabelle Greene with Andy Neumann, Architect, Overall garden courtyard pool, Santa Barbara

LOVELACE GARDEN: A Secluded Oasis

Beautiful flowering plants in baskets and tubs greet the visitor at the entrance door to the Lovelace estate, and convey the feeling that this place is lived in and being loved. An herbaceous border, displaying an unbelievable variety of flowers, winds itself like a garland along the house, and then trails off to rim the wide, open lawn. Here an enormous oak tree reminds the privileged viewer that this is California, not England.

All is walled in by the natural wilderness of tall pine and oak trees, but they have more of a sheltering than restricting effect. I stride along on shady, narrow walkways that slow my footfalls unconsciously to an amble, until the unexpected sight of a large pool, bordered by big sandstones, takes my breath away. How peaceful it all is. You are hardly aware that there is another world, full of haste and noise.

Only the softly cooing call of a pigeon and the determined hammering of a woodpecker can be heard. You could even forget about people—until you detect a tree house hidden among the pines, and a string with a burst balloon, tethered to a twig, which reminds you that this peaceful oasis has been created for a family to enjoy.

OVERALL GARDEN: A Rocky Creation

Looking up and surveying this imposing cliff wall, interspersed with chaparral vegetation and a beautiful flow of stairs—such a harmonious accommodation of nature, design, and function—I suddenly realize that the idea of rocks as something hard, cold, and hostile, ready to crush you, has here transcended to an entirely different meaning.

This garden flows freely into the surrounding wild terrain with no obvious border or separation from the native chaparral. A long, undulating staircase, chiseled out of the mountain wall, cascades downwards until it comes to a stop in something like a courtyard, which is encircled by three wings of the house. Here the large rocks make space for a most beautiful and unusual small pool. Patches of water lilies and fish share its clear water, which comes out of a crack in the cliff higher up and falls in radiating patterns over several rocky surfaces until it spurts into the pool.

Reluctantly I leave. Following another path of rock-
hewn stairs in which succulents nestle in corners and
wild native plants soften its sides, I come to the front
plateau below the house.

Here is a swimming pool of a most impressive style. Shaped in a unique form, also designed by Greene, its wide expanse of water runs smoothly down its rim without forming a ripple, like satin cloth flowing over the edge of a table.

PETERSEN GARDEN: The Sylvan Eden

It is as if the sun-bathed peak of the mountain range had let all its natural abundance slip down until it came to a stop in the Petersen's garden. The golden mountain peak, which seems to loom in remote majesty, not only forms an awe-inspiring backdrop to the estate, but also conveys an atmosphere of peace—the stillness of a sanctuary.

Passing through a handsome wrought iron gate, incorporated into the design by Isabelle Greene, and before proceeding on the uphill drive, I come across a most impressive and unusual swimming pool area. Low golden sandstone walls frame the water, which reflects the sky, the large native trees, and the flagstones. Isabelle Greene's initials are carved into some of the slabs.

Wandering uphill through a shady oak forest, I find Greene's love and respect for the natural landscape so much in evidence. Trees, which established their existence long before this whole area was inhabited by newcomers, remain unthreatened by chainsaw or axe. They form the foundation and give shelter to chaparral vegetation and other shade plants which require little irrigation.

A more open area has flowers, grasses, and bushes in great profusion. Rocks in all shapes and sizes escalate down a shallow slope, where I suddenly detect a small brook quietly wending its way between reeds and moisture-loving plants. Every few steps it forms a shallow pool, which trickles over, disappears under some rocks, and then flows gently again beneath a bank of glowing heucheras and white irises.

Nothing seems to be forced or manicured, yet there is harmony, flow, and order in all this exuberance. The idea of a Garden of Eden comes into my mind—are we missing the animals? You may think so, until you discover a few, also designed by Greene, perching on water faucets and pipes, humorously doing their bit to harmonize nature and these mechanical necessities.

PULITZER GARDEN: Adapted to Personal Needs

To design a grand garden for a person who suffers the sad affliction of being allergic to the pollen of flowers must be a very daunting challenge. Here Isabelle Greene shows again her amazing ingenuity and imagination.

This garden is different from the others I visited. It is very formal, and gives as a whole the impression of a large, sophisticated sculpture. Concrete walls and structures are dominant, but their sterility is softened by a great variety of clipped green bushes, bamboo, reeds, and succulents, all of which grow in beds layered with handsome, smooth pebbles. A series of unusually shaped reflecting pools and basins with overflowing fountains are the first striking features one encounters on entering the estate.

Walled enclosures reveal a cacti terrain, where agaves and aloes, not wedged in with other plants, display their beautiful symmetry and shapes to full advantage. Rocks, again in their natural forms, relieve the stark arrangement of order and formality, while smaller ones along each path conceal built-in electric bulbs that turn on at dusk. With a smile of recognition, I come across a quail, or another little cast iron creature, crowning in their whimsical importance every water faucet and sprinkler.

VALENTINE GARDEN: Climate Adapted Garden

From the balcony of the house, the garden layout appears like a patchwork quilt in a random and imaginative design. Thoughtfully adapted to our semi-arid climate, this happy, colorful carpet is anything but the expected barren desert scenery. There is such a playful abundance of color. Small succulents occupy the narrow gaps between the warm-toned stone slaps; tiny rosettes of them embrace each rock like daisy chains. A big sandstone rock allows a small stonecrop to nestle in its crack, giving its roots room and nourishment. Other rocks interrupt pathways as if by natural placement. Textured walls form a quiet background for elegantly shaped small palms, agaves, and fig trees. Handsome hollyhock stalks in pink bloom prevent these walls from looking too austere.

A raised bed lined by a low wall of sculpted, colored concrete gives the charming impression of a childlike spirit at work: here a variety of lush vegetable plants share the same soil and mingle in perfect harmony with roses, poppies, and many other flowers.

Among this abundance of bright colors rests a large, irregularly-cut slab of shiny gray granite—a natural mirror for the sky. What an ingenious solution to creating a reflecting pool without consuming any water!

The entranced visitor who wanders through this charming domain to the north side of the house comes upon yet another delightful surprise on discovering a small, beautifully designed lily pond, wedged between two walls. How soothing it is to the eye and mind in its quiet setting and stillness.

ISABELLE GREENE: Biography and Selected Project List

EDUCATION

1934   Born in Pasadena (Isabelle Clara McElwain)

1956   B.A. in Botany (California flora emphasis)
       University of California, Los Angeles

1964-69 Coursework towards B.A. in Studio Art (painting, printmaking, sculpture, ceramics)
       University of California, Santa Barbara

1966-70 Private lessons in drawing and painting with Michael Dvortsak

1976   Coursework in Landscape Design and Site Analysis
       University of Oregon, Eugene

1978-82 Landscape Architecture Certification Courses
       University of California, Los Angeles, Extension Program

1982   Certification as Landscape Architect, State of California

BOTANICAL DRAWING PRACTICE

1959-65 Research publications

LANDSCAPE PRACTICE

1964-74 Isabelle C. Haller, Landscape Designer

1974-82 Associate with Michael C. Wheelwright, Landscape Architect

1982-   Principal, Isabelle C. Greene & Associates, Inc., Landscape Architect

SELECTED PROJECTS

Isabelle Greene's projects currently number over five hundred. The following list is a selection of her most significant works. Dates represent initial commission. All locations are in California unless otherwise noted. Asterisked (*) projects represent works in progress as of 2005. Bulleted (•) projects represent structures originally designed by Greene & Greene.

1964	Santa Barbara Psychiatric Clinic (architectural consultant)	Santa Barbara
1966	John and Vicky Alexander (Hunt-Stanbach) Residence Restoration	Santa Barbara
1967	McDermott-Crockett and Associates Mortuary	Santa Barbara
1967	Ralph and Jane Philbrick Residence	Santa Barbara
1969	Mrs. Price Paschall Residence	Santa Barbara
1969	Mr. and Mrs. Holland Residence	Santa Barbara

1969	Solimar Sands Condominiums (Ralph D'Agostino, Architect)	Santa Barbara
1969	Stow House Grounds and Master Planning	Goleta
1970	Mr. and Mrs. Harold S. Gladwin, Esq. Residence	Solvang
1970	Singing Springs Condominiums (Ralph D'Agostino, Architect)	Santa Barbara
1972	Ed and Allice Aspinwall Residence	Santa Barbara
1972	Polly and Warren Tremaine Residence (Paul Gray, Architect)	Santa Barbara
1972	Jon and Lillian Lovelace Residence	Santa Barbara
1975	Polly and Gus Powers Residence	Tampa, FL
1976	Jean de Muller Residence (architectural detailing)	Santa Barbara
1977	All Saints Church (architectural consultant)	Santa Barbara
1977	Raoul and Trudi Schumacher Residence	Santa Barbara
1978	Letty Delany-Failing Residence Restoration	Santa Barbara
1978	Toni and Lazlo Kiraly Residence	Santa Barbara
1979	John and Zola Rex Residence (John Rex, Architect)	Santa Barbara
1980	Carol Lapham Valentine Residence (Paul Gray, Architect)	Santa Barbara
1981	Dayton and Ruth Kieswetter Residence (Roger Phillips, Architect)	Santa Barbara
1981	Leinie Schilling-Mullin Residence	Santa Barbara
1982	Nina and Noah Liff Residence (Warner Gray, Architect)	Santa Barbara
1982	Oak Trail Ranch for Brentwood Association (architectural consultant)	Santa Ynez
1982	Happy Canyon Ranch for Sandy and Heloise Power (Paul Gray, Architect)	Santa Barbara
1982	Bob and Betty Klausner Residence	Santa Barbara
1983	Jim and Ellie Langer Residence	Santa Barbara
1983	Walter and Mara Kohn Residence	Santa Barbara
1984	Nick and Patti Weber Residence (Andy Neumann, Architect)	Santa Barbara
1985	La Casita del Arroyo Public Demonstration Garden for Garden Club of America, Pasadena Chapter (including architectural alterations)	Pasadena
1985	Las Brises Single Family Detached Homes for A-M Company (architectural consultant)	Santa Barbara
1985	Harriett and Jim Fullerton Residence	Carpinteria
1986	Bob and Kelly Witt Residence	Santa Ynez
1986	Ellen and Gregory Brumfiel Residence and Art Gallery	Santa Barbara

1986	Eva and Yoel Haller Residence	Santa Barbara
1986	Little Theatre Restoration for Ganna Walska Lotusland	Santa Barbara
1987	Jack and Reggie Hoag Residence	Santa Barbara
1987	Jim and Amanda McIntyre Residence	Carpinteria
1987	Silver Garden, Glass House Display Garden, Longwood Gardens	Kennett Square, PA
1988	Fran Larkin Residence (Dennis Woodson, Architect)	Carpinteria
1988	George and Marilyn Brumder (Spinks House•) Residence Restoration	Pasadena
1989	Jon and Lillian Lovelace Residence Restoration	Beverly Hills
1991	Joseph Socolich Residence	Huntsville, AL
1991	Don and Marylou Crocker Residence (Karen Clayton, Architect)	Carpinteria
1992	Paul and Leslie Ridley-Tree Residence	Santa Barbara
1992	Ralph and Bonnie Shapira Residence (Peter Becker, Architect)	Malibu
1992	Bruce and Nancy Berman Residence (Gary Jensen, Architect)	Santa Barbara
1993	Bill and June Prindle Residence	Santa Barbara
1993	Reece and Suzanne Duca Residence (Paul Tuttle, Designer)	Carpinteria
1993	Warren/Witt Remodel for Fred and Robin Warren Residence	Santa Ynez
1994	QAD, Inc. Office Headquarters (Andy Neumann, Architect)	Carpinteria
1994	Matt and Karen Yonally Residence (Mark Shield, Architect)	Goleta
1994	Victoria Jackson and Bill Guthy Residence (Andy Neumann, Architect)	Santa Barbara
1994	Harvey and Ellen Knell (Blacker House•) Residence Restoration	Pasadena
1995	Robert and Maria Kelly (T.S. Green House•) Residence Remodel (architectural lead)	Sacramento
1996	Don and Jody Petersen Residence (William La Voie, Architect)	Santa Barbara
1996	Santa Barbara Botanic Garden (Doug Singletary, B₃ Architects)	Santa Barbara
1997	Grand Californian Hotel for Walt Disney Corporation (Peter Dominick, Architect)	Anaheim
1997	Skirball Cultural Center (Moshe Safdie, Architect)	Los Angeles
1997	Tod Birns and Rich Hughes Residence	Santa Barbara
1998	Jack and Sheri Overall Residence (Andy Neumann, Architect)	Santa Barbara
1998	Michael and Ceil Pulitzer Residence (including architectural remodel)	Santa Barbara
1999	University Art Museum, UCSB (Levin & Associates, Architect)	Santa Barbara
1999	Ken and Beth Kaplan Karmin Residence (architectural consultant)	Pacific Palisades

1999	Lynn Stewart Residence	Santa Barbara
1999	Corinna Cotsen and Lee Rosenbaum Residence (Katherine Spetner, Architect)	Santa Monica
2000	Casa Romantica Cultural Center Restoration, Expansion and Demonstration Gardens for the City of San Clemente (Anthony Stark, Architect)	San Clemente
2002	Polly Duxbury Residence*	Santa Ynez
2003	Habitat For Humanity* (Vadim Hsu, Architect)	Santa Barbara
2003	Phillip and Jane Johnston Residence	Santa Barbara
2003	Philip and Carolyn Wyatt Residence	Goleta
2003	John Lesher and Christina Liao Residence* (Barbara Bestor, Architect)	Santa Barbara
2003	Paul Blake and Mark Bennette Residence*	Santa Barbara
2003	Dorothy Largay and Wayne Rosing Residence* (Andy Neumann, Architect)	Santa Barbara
2004	Susan Tai and David Wong Restoration Residence*	Santa Barbara
2004	Nello Gonfiantini Residence* (Carlos Zapata, Architect)	Verdi, NY
2004	Santa Barbara Museum of Natural History Watershed Restoration Project for Community Environmental Council, and Master Planning*	Santa Barbara

Isabelle Haller (Greene)
Lovelace garden swimming pool,
Santa Barbara
Model, clay on wood, 1972

"The Apple Tree Fence Idea," *Sunset* 186 (January 1991): 52-53.

Baldon, Cleo and Ib Melchior, *Reflections on the Pool, California Designs for Swimming* (New York: Rizzoli, 1997), 12-17 [Lovelace], 22-23 [Oak Trail].

Bolton, John, "Mediterranean Magic: The Subtle Beauty and Sensibility of Drought-Tolerant Gardens," *Santa Barbara Magazine* 16 (May-June 1990): 38-40 [Valentine].

Bree, Carmen, "Three Magical Gardens," *Santa Barbara Magazine* 13 (May-June 1987): 34-37 [Lovelace].

Brookes, John, *Garden Masterclass* (London: Dorling Kindersley, 2002), 26-27 [Lovelace], 139, 157, 181 [Valentine], 299 [Longwood], 320 [Liff].

Chamberlin, Susan, "Shades of Gray," *Los Angeles Times Home Magazine* (April 1, 1990) [Fullerton].

Chandler, Philip E., "Spring in Santa Barbara," *Pacific Horticulture* 45 (Winter 1984): 31-37 [Lovelace, Valentine].

Chase, John, "Artistic Earthscape: The Native Palette, Artfully Applied," *Landscape Architecture* 79 (June 1989): 64-68 [Valentine, La Casita del Arroyo, Las Brisas, Langer].

Clifford, Frank, "Dry Landscapes May Give New Meaning to Greening of Los Angeles," *Los Angeles Times* (February 24, 1991).

Conran, Terence and Dan Pearson, *The Essential Garden Book: Getting Back to Basics* (New York: Three Rivers Press, 1998), 45, 126 [Valentine].

Cooper, Paul, *Gardens without Boundaries* (London: Mitchell Beazley, 2003), 62 [Happy Canyon], 140 [Jackson-Guthy].

Cox, Rachel S., "Serendipity and Symbolism: The Gardens of Isabelle Greene," *Garden Design* 11 (December 1991): 42-49 [Liff, Larkin, Hoag].

Crotta, Carol A., "Garden Artistry," *Home Magazine* 35 (January 1989): 54-59 [Liff, Lovelace, Valentine].

Crouch, DeAnne Musof, "Shades of Greene," *Santa Barbara News-Press Woman Magazine* (June 4, 2000).

De Long, James, "A True Story-Book House: Begins a Fourth Life as a Designer's Home," *House Beautiful* 114 (October 1972): 104-109 [Alexander].

"Design for Private Living: A Compact One-Level Plan for Safety and Easy Maintenance," *House and Garden* 148 (April 1976): 118-121 [Tremaine].

Dobrin, Arnold, "Pools for Many Purposes," *Los Angeles Times Home Magazine* (March 1, 1981) [Lovelace].

Dunn, Teri Blau, "Fields of Succulents, Rivers of Stone," *Horticulture* 67 (August 1989): 31-37 [Valentine].

"Escape to the Pool House," *Home Magazine* 32 (September 1986): 87-88 [Lovelace].

Fowler, Veronica Lorson, *Garden Pools and Fountains* (San Ramon, CA: Ortho Books, 1988), 78, 81, 89 [Liff].

Frieze, Charlotte M., "Garden Under Glass: at Longwood, Silver Shines," *Connoisseur* 219 (June 1989): 124-128.

Frieze, Charlotte M., *Social Gardens: Outdoor Spaces for Living and Entertaining* (New York: Stuart, Tabori & Chang, Inc., 1988), 75, 108, 109, 166-167, 169-170 [Happy Canyon, Liff, Valentine].

Greenberg, Cara, "Field of Dreams," *House Beautiful* 135 (April 1993): 188-122 [Greene's submission for barren plot surrounding house in Tuscaloosa, Alabama].

Greene, Isabelle, "Foreword," in Kevin Connelly, *Month by Month in a Waterwise Garden* (Los Angeles: Historical Society of Southern California, 1991).

Greene, Isabelle, "Introduction," in Elizabeth Vogt, *Montecito: California Garden Paradise* (Montecito, CA: MIP Publishers 1993).

Greene, Isabelle, "Mediterranean Gardening: The Benefits and Challenges of Slim Rainfall," *The Mediterranean Garden* 22 (October 2000): 58-59.

Greene, Isabelle, "A New Division: The Spatial Arts," *Santa Barbara Arts Magazine* 2 (1987): 5-8.

Greene, Isabelle, "Tiny Drops: A Lifeline for Trees," *Los Angeles Times* (July 22, 1990).

Greene, Isabelle with Elizabeth Vogt, "My Grandfather, Henry Mather Greene," *Pasadena Magazine* (Winter 1994): 13-15.

Hayward, Gordon, *Garden Paths: A New Way to Solve Practical Problems in the Garden* (Boston: Houghton Mifflin, 1998), 101-102 [Valentine].

Heeger, Susan, "Gardens: The Hard Stuff, It's Easy to Plant a Lyrical Landscape, but Designers See Beauty in a Garden's Built Form as Well," *Los Angeles Times Magazine* (October 23, 1994).

Heeger, Susan, "Second Nature," *Los Angeles Times Magazine* (February 22, 1998) [Duca].

"Just Desert," *The Sunday Telegraph Magazine* (June 13, 1999) [Valentine].

"Landscape Architect, Designer Join Forces," *Santa Barbara News-Press* (April 21, 1974).

"Landscaping at Clinic Lauded," *Santa Barbara News-Press* (October 31, 1966) [Santa Barbara Psychiatric Clinic].

Leccese, Michael, "Opposites Attract," *Landscape Architecture* 86 (May 1996): 30, 32-37 [Duca].

Leviseur, Elsa, "Avant-garde Ecology," *Architectural Review* 191 (September 1992): 53-58 [Valentine].

Logan, William Bryant, "Conquering a California Hillside," *House & Garden* 159 (July 1987): 90-99, 186-189 [Valentine].

Muller, Walter H., *Botany: A Functional Approach* (New York: MacMillan Co., 1963) [selected illustrations by Isabelle C. Haller].

Otis, Denise, *Grounds for Pleasure, Four Centuries of the American Garden* (New York: Harry N. Abrams, 2002), 326-329 [Valentine].

Otis, Denise, "New American Garden: Digging for a California Style," *House & Garden* 164 (November 1992): 189-195.

Pereire, Anita, *Gardens for the Twenty First Century* (London: Aurum, 1999), 187-189 [Oak Trail, Lovelace, Berman].

Power, Nancy Goslee, Susan Heeger, and Mick Hales, *The Gardens of California: Four Centuries of Design from Mission to Modern* (New York: C. Potter, 1995), 75, 84-87, 157, 168-171 [Lovelace, Valentine].

"The Shape of Motion," *House & Garden* (January 1997): 118-125 [Valentine].

Sims, Burt, "Casa Romantica," *South Coast* (Summer 2001): 44-45.

Smaus, Robert, "Fall Planting: The Shrinking Lawn. Southern California's Most Forward Thinking Landscape Architects and Designers Face the Challenge of Limited Water," *Los Angeles Times Home Magazine* (October 2, 1988).

Smaus, Robert, "Breaking Ground: Permeable Paving Provides Greenery in Unexpected Places," *Los Angeles Times Magazine* (October 30, 1988) [La Casita del Arroyo].

Stevens, David, *Roof Gardens, Balconies and Terraces* (New York: Rizzoli, 1997), 35, 83, 91, 103, 110 [Valentine].

Suttro, Dirk, "Shades of Greene," *Garden Design* 12 (May/June 1993): 48-53 [Baumes].

Thompson, Elspeth and Melanie Eclare, *New Decorated Garden* (New York: Ryland Peters & Small, 2002), 60-61, 76-77, 79, 88-89, 94b, 134a, 134b, 134-135, 136b [Valentine].

Trulove, James Grayson, ed., *The New American Garden: Innovations in Residential Landscape Architecture: 60 Case Studies* (New York: Whitney Library of Design, 1998), 70-79 [Duca, Oak Trail, Valentine].

Waterman, Pamela, "Isabelle Greene: Botanist, Artist, and Landscape Architect," *Pacific Horticulture* 65 (July/Aug/Sept 2004): 17-25.

Weller, Bonnie, "Longwood's Silver Garden," *Philadelphia Inquirer* (April 16, 1989).

White, Hazel, *Small Patios: Simple Projects, Contemporary Designs* (San Francisco: Chronicle Books, 2001), 10-11, 31, 61-21, 86-88 [Petersen, Valentine].

White, Hazel, *Small Tree Gardens: Simple Projects, Contemporary Designs* (San Francisco: Chronicle Books, 2000) [Duca, Petersen, Valentine].

Isabelle Greene, Valentine garden, Santa Barbara

Notes on Contributors

ISABELLE C. GREENE is a granddaughter of Henry Mather Greene, and grandniece of Charles Sumner Greene, partners in the important California Arts-and-Crafts architectural firm, Greene and Greene. Trained as a botanist and artist, Greene began work in Santa Barbara as a landscape designer in 1964. Since 1982, she has been principal of the Santa Barbara firm, Isabelle C. Greene & Associates, Inc. Greene has completed over five hundred landscape projects, a number of which have included architectural designs. Her pioneering landscapes in California and elsewhere in the United States have helped to focus attention on the need for environmentally sensitive and sustainable design. She is a recipient of numerous awards, including the American Horticulture Society's Landscape Design Award in 1995, and is a Fellow of the American Society of Landscape Architects.

KURT G.F. HELFRICH has been curator of the Architecture and Design Collection at the University Art Museum, University of California, Santa Barbara since 1997. He is an architectural historian specializing in nineteenth and twentieth-century American and European art and design. He has curated exhibitions on Southern California designers Sam Reisbord, Maynard Lyndon, Barton Myers, Lutah Maria Riggs, and John Elgin Woolf, among others. His publications include essays on the R.M. Schindler archive, the architectural projects of the Santa Barbara furniture designer Paul Tuttle, and the development of Santa Barbara's civic core around Plaza de la Guerra beginning in the 1920s. He is currently working with the University of Pennsylvania's Architectural Archives in preparation for a retrospective exhibition and catalogue examining the work of the twentieth-century designers Antonin and Noémi Raymond in Japan and the United States.

INES ROBERTS has lived in Santa Barbara since 1966 and is self-taught in photography. She is the author of thirty-five slide/music shows, all of which were premiered at the Santa Barbara Museum of Art. Her photographs have won many prizes both in the United States and abroad. She is a Fellow of the Royal Photographic Society of Great Britain and was invited to be a member of the London Salon of Photography. Her prints and articles have been published widely. In 2003, the *BBC Wildlife Magazine* and the Natural History Museum of London accorded her the title Wildlife Photographer of the Year, in the category of Wild Places.

KAREN SINSHEIMER is curator of Photography at the Santa Barbara Museum of Art. In her fourteen-year tenure she has organized over ten traveling exhibitions, shown in both national and international venues, each accompanied by a major publication. She is currently at work on the fifth exhibition, in a series of six, focused on photography of the nineteenth century.

DAVID C. STREATFIELD is a professor of Landscape Architecture and Urban Design and Planning at the University of Washington. His research interests include the history of modern landscape design in Europe and the United States from the eighteenth century to the present. He is the author of *California Gardens: Creating a New Eden* (1994) and several essays published in books and scholarly journals. He is also active in historic preservation.

HAZEL WHITE is a freelance writer who has written extensively on Isabelle Greene's landscape designs. She is the author of ten books and an award-winning newspaper column. She lives in San Francisco.

Exhibition Checklist

All dimensions are in inches, height by width by depth. Unless otherwise noted, all drawings are delineated by Isabelle Greene.
All works are courtesy of Isabelle C. Greene & Associates, Inc.

1. Santa Barbara Psychiatric Clinic Garden, Santa Barbara, CA (1964-66)

Working Drawings

Entrance Elevation (n.d.) graphite and oil pastel on paper on board (12 x 25)

Landscape Plan: Front Area (n.d.) graphite on tracing paper (16 x 34.75)

Landscape Plan: North Patio (n.d.) graphite on tracing paper (12 x 18)

2. Lovelace Residence Garden, Santa Barbara, CA (1972-73; 1989-91; 2000)

Sketches

Elevation of Poolside Rock Bank (n.d.) graphite on tracing paper (8.5 x 11)

Driveway Plant List (1972) graphite on tracing paper (11 x 17)

Terrace Border: Perennials and Some Annuals (October 1972) graphite on vellum (16.5 x 37)

Driveway Revisions: Plan (2000) graphite on vellum (12 x 20.75)

Working Drawings

Swimming Pool: Plot Plan (1973) graphite on vellum (20.75 x 30.5)

Swimming Pool: Details (1973) graphite on vellum (18.5 x 29.25)

Driveway Plan (1973) graphite on vellum (25.25 x 36)

Model

Pool Model (1972) clay on wood (6.25 x 10.75 x 1.5)

3. Tremaine Residence Garden, Santa Barbara, CA (1972-73)

Sketches:

Preliminary Site Plan (n.d) graphite on tracing paper (12 x 15.25)

Working Drawings

Landscape Plan (1973) graphite on vellum (17 x 22)

Tree Wells, Sections, and Elevations (n.d) graphite on vellum (17 x 22)

4. Valentine Residence Garden, Santa Barbara, CA (1980-84)

Sketches

Terrace Plans (n.d.) [3 sheets] graphite on tracing paper (12 x 16; 12 x 18.5; 12 x 20)

Working Drawings

Plan: Irrigation, Drainage Requirements (1982) graphite on vellum
[delineated by Steve Goggia] (24 x 36)

Landscape Construction: Sections and Elevations (1983) graphite and colored pencil on vellum
[delineated by Steve Goggia] (24 x 36)

Zen Garden: Plan and Elevations (1983) graphite on vellum (24 x 36)

5. Oak Trail Ranch Garden for the Brentwood Association, Santa Ynez, CA (1982-83)

Sketches

Site Plan (1982) graphite on tracing paper (18 x 36.5)

Pool: Preliminary Sketches (n.d.) graphite on tracing paper (16.5 x 17.5)

Working Drawings

Plan: Lawn Extensions and Additions (1983) graphite on vellum (24 x 36)

6. Weber Residence Garden, Santa Barbara, CA (1984-98)

Sketches

Site Plan: Phase 1 Color Garden (1984) graphite on tracing paper (18 x 24)

Working Drawings

Planting Plan (1998) graphite and colored pencil on vellum
[delineated by Bethany Clough and Isabelle Greene] (24 x 36)

Plan: Color Garden for Dining Room (1985) graphite on tracing paper on vellum (24 x 36)

7. La Casita del Arroyo Public Demonstration Garden for the Garden Club of America, Pasadena Chapter, Pasadena, CA (1985-95)

Sketches

Clubhouse Elevation (n.d.) felt tip pen on vellum (8.5 x 11)

Clubhouse Elevations (1985) [2 sheets] graphite on vellum (8.5 x 11)

Site Plan: Schematic Proposal (1986) graphite on graph paper (30 x 76.5)

Gate Concept Plan (1993) graphite on vellum (22.75 x 12)

Working Drawings

Schematic Driveway Gates and Stonework Alterations (1993) graphite on vellum
[delineated by Heide Baldwin and Isabelle Greene] (24 x 36)

Water Conservation Garden Signage (n.d.) electrostatic print on paper (22.75 x 11)

8. Silver Garden, Glass House Display Garden, Longwood Gardens, Kennett Square, PA (1987-88)

Sketches

Ceiling Treatments: Schemes A, B (1987) graphite on tracing paper (9 x 11)

Perspective Looking into House #22 (1987) graphite on vellum (24 x 15.25)

Interior Perspectives: Looking Towards Acacia House Doors; Looking at Banana House Door (1987) graphite on vellum (9 x 12)

Planters (1987) {3 sheets] graphite on vellum (9 x 12)

Olive Tree Weights (1989) graphite on vellum (11 x 17)

Working Drawings

Preliminary Landscape Plan (1988) graphite on vellum
[delineated by Jane Duncan and Isabelle Greene] (24 x 36)

"A Grey and Silver Garden" Cover Sheet (1988) graphite on vellum (24 x 36)

9. Larkin Residence Garden, Carpinteria, CA (1988-90)

Sketches:

Site Plan (1993) graphite and watercolor on paper (16 x 12)

Working Drawings

As-Built Planting Plan (1990) graphite on vellum
[delineated by Heide Baldwin] (24 x 36.25)

As-Built Planting Plan (1990) graphite on vellum
[delineated by Heide Baldwin] (24 x 36.25)

10. Petersen Residence Garden, Santa Barbara, CA (1996-2002)

Working Drawings

Conceptual Landscape Plan (1996) graphite on vellum
[delineated by Isabelle Greene, Maury Plunkett] (24 x 36)

Garden Pool: Plan (1997-99) graphite and colored pencil on vellum
[delineated by John Hreno] (24 x 36)

Garden Pool: Elevations (1998-1999) graphite on vellum
[delineated by John Hreno] (24.5 x 36)

Preliminary Planting Plan: Pool Area (1999) graphite and colored pencil on vellum
[delineated by Bethany Clough and Isabelle Greene] (24 x 36)

11. Pulitzer Residence Garden, Santa Barbara, CA (1998)

Sketches

Site Plan (n.d.) graphite on tracing paper (30.5 x 23)

12. Overall Residence Garden, Santa Barbara, CA (1998-2001)

Sketches

Site Plan: Pool to Road (n.d.) graphite on tracing paper (19.5 x 31)

Site Plan: Guest House Path (n.d.) graphite on tracing paper (19.5 x 21)

Working Drawings

Preliminary Site Plan (1998) graphite on vellum
[delineated by Bethany Clough and Isabelle Greene] (29 x 45)

Planting Plan: Upper Slope (1999) graphite on vellum
[delineated by Jack Harris and Karin Kaufmann] (24 x 36)

Planting Plan: Middle Area (2001) graphite and colored pencil on vellum
[delineated by Karin Kaufmann and Jason Lee] (24 x 36)

Planting Plan: Guesthouse and Vicinity (2001) graphite on vellum
[delineated by Isabelle Greene, Karin Kaufmann, and Jason Lee] (24 x 36)

Isabelle Greene, Lovelace garden, Santa Barbara

PHOTOGRAPHY CREDITS

All images are provided by and reproduced with the permission of the following individuals.

William B. Dewey—26, 30 bottom

Isabelle C. Greene—cover background, 27, 28, 32 middle, bottom, 33, 34 bottom, 42, 45, 46, 50, 51, 52, 53, 55, 56, 57, 85, 95, 96

C. Mick Hales—cover inset

Jerry Harpur—37

Timothy Hearsum—1, 38

Gregory Heisler—40

Saxon Holt—29, 32 top

Neumann Mendro Andrulaitis, Architects—48

Ines Roberts—2, 5, 8, 9, 30 top, 34 top, 39, 58, 61, 62, 63, 64, 65, 66, 67, 68, 69, 70, 71, 72, 73, 74, 75, 76, 77, 78, 79, 80, 81, 88, 93, 94

David C. Streatfield—10, 12, 16 middle, bottom, 17, 19, 21, 22, 23

Tim Street-Porter—16 top

LIBRARY OF CONGRESS CATALOGING-IN-PUBLICATION DATA

Helfrich, Kurt Gerard Frederick.

Isabelle Greene : shaping place in the landscape
/ Kurt G. F. Helfrich ; with contributions by Isabelle Greene ... [et al.].

p. cm.

Catalog of an exhibition held March 30-May 15, 2005.

Includes bibliographical references.

ISBN 0-942006-73-9 (pbk.)

1. Greene, Isabelle Clara, 1934---Exhibitions. 2. Landscape architects--California--Biography--Exhibitions. 3. Landscape architecture--California--Exhibitions. I. Title: Shaping place in the landscape. II. Greene, Isabelle Clara, 1934- III. University of California, Santa Barbara. University Art Museum. IV. Title.

SB470.G74H45 2005

712'.092--dc22   2005004210

Isabelle Greene with Andy Neumann, Architect, Overall garden courtyard pool, Santa Barbara

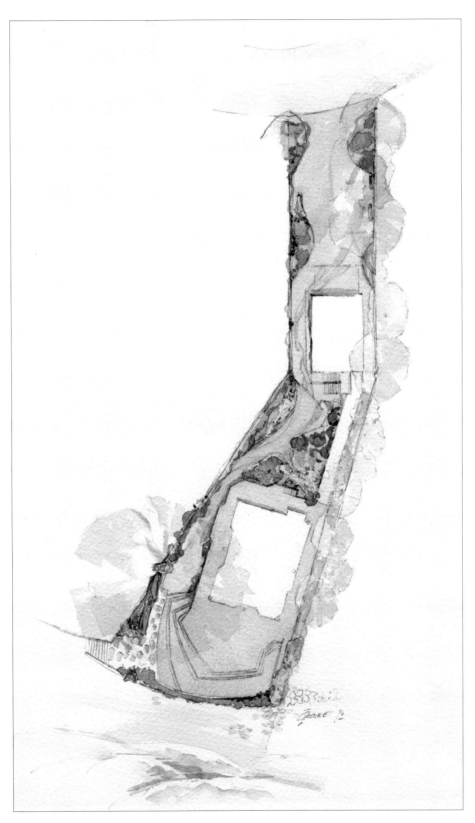

Isabelle Greene with Dennis Woodson, Architect, Larkin garden, Carpinteria
Site Plan, graphite and watercolor on paper, 1993

To stand
with sunlight on my eyelids

Is to stand
within the radiance
of paradise.

Isabelle Greene, 2002

Isabelle Greene, New Orleans, 1990